RACECOURSES
ON THE FLAT

RACECOURSES
ON THE FLAT

JOHN TYRREL

THE CROWOOD PRESS

First published in 1989 by
THE CROWOOD PRESS
Ramsbury, Marlborough
Wiltshire SN8 2HE

Printed and bound by Richard Clay Ltd, Bungay
Typeset in 10/13 pt Plantin Light by
Pindar (Scotland) Limited, Edinburgh.

British Library Cataloguing in Publication Data
Tyrrel, John
    Racecourses on the flat.
    1. Great Britain. Racecourses, to 1983
    I. Title
    798.4'006'841

    ISBN 1-85223-268-4

For Ginny

Hamilton Park ■   ■ Edinburgh

■ Ayr

■ Newcastle

Carlisle ■

Catterick ■   ■ Redcar
■ Thirsk

Ripon ■   ■ York

■ Beverley

Pontefract ■

Haydock Park ■   ■ Doncaster

Chester ■

■ Nottingham

■ Leicester

Wolverhampton ■

■ Yarmouth

Warwick ■

■ Newmarket

Chepstow ■

Ascot

Windsor ■   ■ Sandown

Bath ■

Newbury ■   ■ Epsom   Lingfield

Salisbury ■   Kempton   ■ Folkestone

Goodwood ■   ■ Brighton

CONTENTS

Acknowledgements

The author is grateful to all who have assisted in the preparation of this book, and in particular to the following: Ann Robinson, Jane Orde-Powlett, Susan Carrol and Candy Whiston of the Thoroughbred Breeders' Association; Sam Sheppard for the loan of books from the TBA Library; Dede Marks, Curator of the York Racing Museum and Library for the loan of books; Margaret Cresswell and Ann Bowden for the loan of books; Mark Kershaw, Nick Cheyne and Michael Webster for the loan of books, material and photographs, together with much advice on Sandown, Kempton and Epsom; Bill and David McHarg for the loan of books and much advice on the Scottish courses; Andrew Franklin, 'the onlie begetter'; Jackie Dennis for typing the manuscript and decyphering the author's writing; Graham Hart for editing and Graeme Murdoch for the design and picture research (with special thanks to Elaine Hart at the Illustrated London News Picture Library); Chris and Jo Forster for their faith, help, advice and encouragement; and finally my wife Virginia, who has had to live for six months with two thousand years of racing memorabilia on the dining room table.

Introduction

IN AN age of increasing standardisation, the flat racecourses of Britain are almost wilfully diverse; it is a cliché of sport to compare them with the uniformity of tracks around the world, notably the Americas. From the extreme undulations of Epsom, to the soup plate circumference of Chester, from the wide galloping heath of Newmarket to the rare loop courses of Salisbury and Hamilton, the British Turf is rich in variety.

Their diversity of shape is matched only by the wealth of their history. As I have attempted to show, they have been shaped by time, both physically and in the cut of their character. They owe their present to the richness of the past, a past littered with great characters – owners, trainers, jockeys, punters and, of course, horses. And in that we enjoy the traditions and quirks of the British racing scene we must all be grateful for those people throughout history who have, quite simply, enjoyed a day at the races. There's something special about it, the sense of which I hope I have conveyed.

This book is not intended to be encyclopaedic, neither is it a history of races, horses or people, although they have their exits and their entrances. Rather, I have hoped to capture the flavour and atmosphere of the past, which is not merely a nostalgic background to the present but so often a guide to the future. Accordingly, I have not dwelt too much on recent times which are still fresh in the mind and which are without the benefit of historical perspective.

For the purposes of the book the courses are organised by region, further than that, alphabetically. I would not want to imply any order of standing among these fine old monuments to British sport although, as the reader will spot, I have devoted more pages to some courses than others.

If the play's the thing, then this is a book about theatres; the playhouses of racing which have been the setting for comedy and drama the like of which most dramatists can only dream about.

John Tyrrel

Winchester, 1989

SALMON TROUT AT HOME AT WHATCOMBE

STEVE DONOGHUE BY MUNNINGS

PERSIMMON'S DERBY, 1896

WINNERS ENCLOSURE, ROYAL ASCOT, 1979

GORDON RICHARDS AND SUN CHARIOT

AYR

'Ye elements, in whose ennobling stir, I feel myself exalted.'

Lord Byron.

A LINE from a poet who spent his early youth in Scotland, describing a scene more familiar to an earlier romantic, Robert Burns. As F.H. Bayles says in his *Race Course Atlas* of 1903, the Ayr Western Meeting is held 'within a short distance of the subject of that pastoral picture immortalised by Robbie Burns, "Ye banks and braes o'bonnie Doon"'.

Bayles goes on to describe the Western Meeting as that 'at which most of the elite of Scotch Society bestow their patronage and supported by drafts of horses from all the principal North country stables. This delightful meeting occupies three days in the week following the great St Leger . . . the meeting, or gathering, as the Scots designate their festivities, is looked forward to by the Scottish Society, who hold large house parties for it. A ball also takes place in conjunction with the meeting on each of the three race nights at the County Hall.'

Having given details of the railway connections so vital in the early days of the motor car, Bayles concludes by describing the sea coast: 'with the apex of Goat's Fell in the Isle of Arran looming in the distance beyond a stretch of lovely marine scenery'.

Little has changed, except for the site of the course itself; Bayles was speaking of the tiny track, no larger than Chester, situated on what is now the Belleisle golf course. Here racing had taken place, probably since 1771 and certainly since 1777 when

first recorded in the *Racing Calendar*, but there was racing at Ayr, or Air, about two hundred years earlier.

Captain Michael Sayers can have had few more unhappy moments in a distinguished career than when attempting to start the 1986 Portland Handicap by flag at Doncaster, and as he bellowed, 'Come back you buggers!' in vain after the disappearing waterproof-clad bottoms of the jockeys who had anticipated his flag-fall, he might have reflected that a starter's lot, like a policeman's, is not always a happy one.

If it is of any compensation to the gallant Captain, things were a whole lot nastier at Ayr in 1576 when a quarrel over the fairness of the start resulted in the starter being shot in the thigh and his assistant in the leg, or so the story goes.

A little less than two centuries later, Sir John Douglas's Phillipo took the honours in the record books as Ayr's first winner. The event was a £50 plate and Phillipo also walked over for another £50 stake at the same two-day meeting.

In 1777, a much grander five-day fixture was staged, in October, with animals rejoicing in the names of Bamboozle, Blemish and Tyger among the winners. The racecourse was then on part of the burgh moor and unenclosed; the route which Tam O'Shanter, as described by Burns in his poem, is supposed to have taken on his ride to Alloway Kirk would have crossed the racetrack, or passed nearby.

About nine years later, Robert Burns became a welcome associate of prominent men of the Turf, notably the Caledonian Hunt Club. Quite how this came about is a little obscure; Burns' best friend

18

would not have described him as a racing man. Perhaps he was captivated by the social side, and more probably by the ladies. Certainly he was much taken with Lady Harriet Don, wife of Sir Alexander Don, whose Forester had won a £50 race on the second day of the 1777 meeting.

In 1787 Burns dedicated a new edition of his poems to the Caledonian Hunt Club, and they in turn became his patrons. One of Burns' most famous songs, *Ye Banks and Braes of Bonnie Doon*, is set to a tune called the *Caledonian Hunt's Delight* and the connection was to last for the rest of the poet's life; as did his friendship with Mrs Frances Dunlop, to whom he confided that the more boisterous of the Caledonians sometimes offended his sensitive temperament.

Burns died in 1796 at the age of thirty-seven, worn out by hard living. His widow was not forgotten by the Caledonians, and one of their number, the Hon. William Maule, gave her an annuity of £50.

The new century brought a new race, the Ayr Gold Cup. As John Fairfax-Blakeborough rightly points out in his *Northern Turf History*, what the St Leger means to Yorkshire, and the Northumberland Plate means to what used to be called Northumberland, the Ayr Gold Cup means to Scotland.

The first race, in 1804, was run in two heats of two miles each. The conditions were for three-year-olds and upwards, and the race confined to horses bred and trained in Scotland; the winner was Chancellor, owned by Lord Cassillis, whose ancestor had been present in 1576 (when they shot unsatisfactory starters).

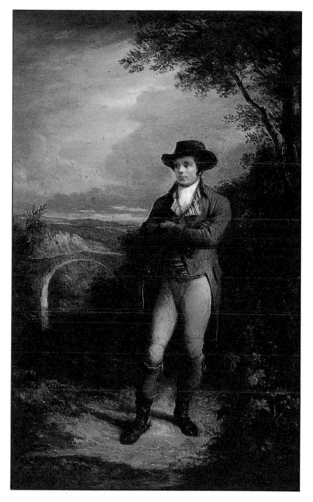

ROBERT BURNS

After Chancellor had won the Gold Cup, he went on the same afternoon to finish second in the next race, the Ayr Subscription of £50 divided into four heats of four miles. So Chancellor managed to lug 8st 10lb over twenty miles in one day at racing pace.

Chancellor won the Ayr Gold Cup again in 1805, and from then on it became what was known as a single heat race, that is to say a straightforward two mile contest. As with all restricted racing, the event became more than a little incestuous, and Lord Eglinton won the race six times between 1809 and 1819. His first winner, Bit of Tartan, was the dam of Sans Culottes, the neatly-named winner of the 1818 Cup. A Mr Ramsay of Barnton owned nine winners from 1835 to 1844, and the stallion John Bull, winner of the 1792 Derby under Frank Buckle and standing at Auchline, near Irvine, sired the first four home in the Cups of 1810 and 1811, as well as the winners of 1812 and 1814.

The Western Meeting Club was formed in 1824 and the first Western Meeting took place that year. The Club inaugurated two-year-old racing at Ayr the following year, with a £25 sweepstakes, £10 forfeit and £50 added for a six furlong race, colts 8st 3lb, fillies 8st. Four went to post and the winner was Sir William Maxwell's Spae-wife.

Prize money at the Western Meeting was £1,440 in 1830, and was nearly £2,000 in 1838 when the programme included a £500 sweepstakes for two-year-olds, half forfeit and worth £1,250 to the winner; this was the richest race in the United Kingdom for juveniles, easily exceeding the £910 Criterion Stakes at Newmarket. The winner was Doctor Caius, ridden by Tommy Lye, and Lord Eglinton's bay went on to win the Ayr Gold Cup in 1840 and twenty-one races in all, many south of the border at Goodwood, Liverpool and Newmarket.

The Cup became a handicap in 1855, and Lerrywheut, ridden by Tommy Aldcroft was first past the post, but the jockey dismounted before reaching the weighing room, and was disqualified. John Dory, the runner-up, was given the race; the next day, they met again in a two-horse race for the Ayrshire Handicap, and the reason for Aldcroft's premature dismount after the Cup became clear, as Lerrywheut broke down and never ran again.

Aldcroft had succeeded Tommy Lye as stable jockey to Tom Dawson at Middleham. Lye was a whip artist, in complete contrast to the considerate style of Aldcroft, who had the difficult role of being the favourite jockey of the irascible Earl of Glasgow. Aldcroft still managed to ride six classic winners in between frequent sackings and re-instatements. He also gained a reputation as a dandy, and claimed to have introduced peg-top trousers into Middleham, doubtless the fashion event of the decade.

Fred Archer made his debut at Ayr in 1872, and the fifteen-year-old apprentice finished second in the Caledonian Handicap on Grace. The next day, his only mount, Alaric, finished almost last in the Ayrshire Handicap, but came out again on the Friday to win the Ayr Gold Cup by ten lengths; the stewards seemed unperturbed by this somewhat inconsistent running.

But time was running out for the old course. Notwithstanding Bayles' delight in both the scenery and the social ambience, he was very critical of a track best described as a right-handed Chester, but here the resemblance seemed to end; there are really no straights on the Roodee, but Ayr had a two-and-a-half furlong gallop on the far side, turning sharply into a run-in of only 470 yards, and many horses ran out on the turn for home; the going was described as 'very lumpy'.

The site was cramped, and modernisation impossible. The only option was to move, and Ayr's card of rich prizes found a new home on the present course in 1907, under the guidance of David Shaw, the Clerk of the Course who had served Ayr for many years and was to continue until his death in 1924.

Four annual fixtures were established by 1908: the Spring Meeting in April, the Summer Meeting

CAPT CHARLES ELSEY ON HIS RETIREMENT WITH SON BILL, 1960

in July, the August Meeting and of course the Western Meeting in September, featuring the Ayr Gold Cup, run for the first time at today's distance of six furlongs.

The winner in 1908 was Raeberry, owned by The Duke of Montrose and ridden by R. Crisp. Whisky was half-a-crown a bottle (carriage paid), a saloon class steamship ticket to America cost £10, and if emigration seemed a little drastic, the Scottish Hagey Company of Glasgow offered to cure your drink habit in three days.

Since trainers were first licensed by the Jockey Club in 1905, Ayr had been a training centre, and the new course on Doonside added to the prosperity of the trainers. Many celebrated names appear. Harry Whiteman, who trained pre-war for Peter Cazalet, trained the Ayr Gold Cup winner

Irish Dance in 1949, ridden by Edgar Britt. Whiteman should also have had the credit for a Grand National winner in 1936, as his Davy Jones, ridden by Mr Anthony (later Lord) Mildmay were well clear when the reins broke and Davy Jones ran out.

Captain Charles Elsey, the last northern trainer to head the championship list (in 1956) trained in the twenties at Clyde House and sent Westmead out to win the Ayr Gold Cup in 1924. But perhaps the most famous name is George Formby, a man who eventually made his reputation in a very different field as an international music hall and film star.

Son of George Formby Snr, who was also a star of comedy and topped the bill on the Edwardian stage with his ukulele act (although quite how an Hawaiian instrument became the hallmark of a Lancashire comedian is lost in time), Formby Jnr was apprenticed at Ayr in 1915 to James Burns, and went with Burns to Ireland in the same year. Going to scale at 6st 5lb, he rode in Eire until 1919, when he joined the Hon. George Lambton at Newmarket. But George's talents clearly lay elsewhere. Like many a man before and since, Formby owed his subsistence to the kindness of the lady who ran the local fish and chip bar, in this case Mrs Pat Kelly, who supplied him with half-price suppers at Ayr when George was earning only a few shillings a week.

There was the inevitable hiatus during the First World War, but racing resumed in 1919 when 'Brownie' Carslake won the Cup on Beresina in the colours of Lord Derby.

The death of David Shaw in 1924 left an administrative vacuum which was difficult to fill. Shaw's son William acted for a time as joint Clerk of the Course with Charles Manning, but soon relinquished the post in favour of Alec McHarg, a member of David Shaw's legal practice in Ayr. The Manning-McHarg partnership ensured that Ayr maintained its position as Scotland's premier course.

Perhaps the most notable event between the wars was the 1936 Gold Cup, when Albert 'Midge' Richardson, one of the finest lightweight jockeys ever seen, weighed out at 6st 13lb to win on Marmaduke Jinks. It was the lowest weight carried to victory since the race was run over six furlongs, and Richardson was not an apprentice, but a fully fledged jockey aged forty-two.

Like many courses, Ayr was taken over by the army for the duration of the 1939-45 war, but racing resumed in 1946, on 17th May. Alec McHarg and Charles Manning continued in office, grappling with the tiresome shortages of the post-war world, until Manning retired in 1949 and Alec McHarg's son, William, joined his father in the joint clerkship.

Alec died in 1956, and Kit Patterson joined Bill McHarg, the man who has done more than any other to promote racing in Scotland. Bill retired in December 1988, but the dynasty continues with his son David in charge.

It is impossible to leave Ayr without paying tribute to a brace of great names of the past: Sir Jack Jarvis and Lord Rosebery. Jarvis won the 1905 Ayr Gold Cup as an apprentice on Kilglass and went on to train 103 winners at the Western Meeting in a career spanning sixty-six years, including 121 victories as a flat race jockey, plus a few under National Hunt Rules.

Many of Jarvis' winners were trained for Lord Rosebery, and his father the fifth Earl; the names of Jarvis and Rosebery are remembered in two-year-old events at the Western Meeting.

The future of Ayr, which also boasts a fine National Hunt course, and is the home of the Scottish Grand National, now seems secure following the proposed sale of the disused Craigie Stand to a supermarket chain. This will finance major rebuilding of the stands and an all-weather exercise track. It may seem a far cry from Robbie Burns to Tesco's, but as the man of verse himself proclaimed:

'The rank is but the guinea's stamp;
The man's the gowd for a'that!' ∎

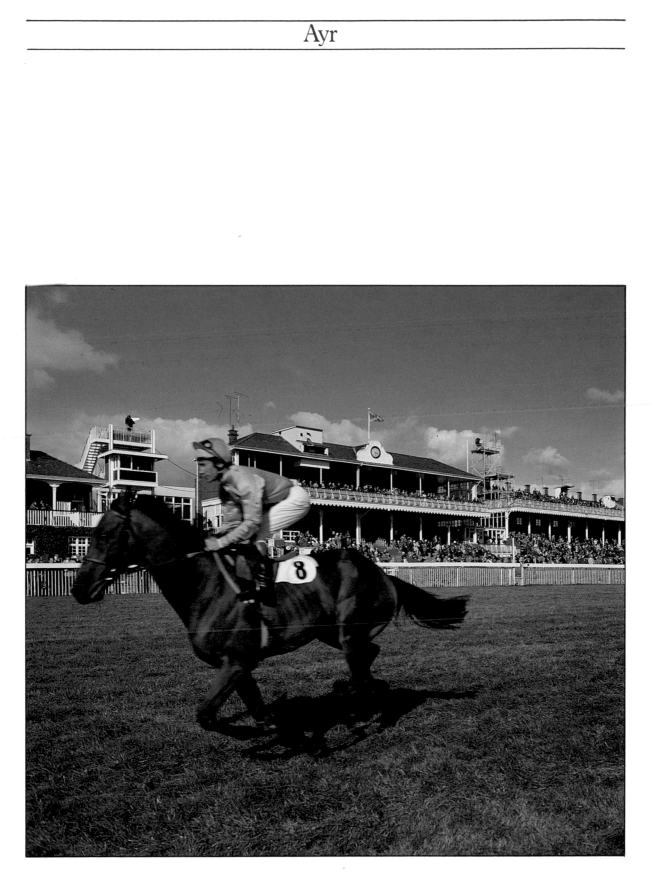

AYR RACES

EDINBURGH

'Now mony a scaw'd and bare-backed loun
Rise early to their work:
Enough to fley a muckle town,
Wi' dinsome squeel and bark,
"Here is the true and faithfu' list
O'Noblemen and Horses;
Their eild, their weight, their height, their
grist,
That rin for plates or purses." '

SO RUNS the fourth verse of the Edinburgh poet Robert Ferguson's twenty-stanza description of Leith Races in 1772. This mention of the hawkers selling racecards is about the kindest thing he has to say about the sports, taking the rather Calvinistic view that drinking and gambling are bad for you, although his moral tale ends on an optimistic note.

Whatever Ferguson may have thought, the Scottish gentry are unlikely to have agreed. As Major John Fairfax-Blakeborough writes in his *Northern Turf History*, during the 1770s and 80s, Edinburgh races were to Scotland what York races were to the north of England. It was an annual gathering of all of 'rank and high degree', many of whom had houses in the city. There was much entertaining at house parties, with all the attendant balls and assemblies and the inevitable cock-fighting. This attracted as much or more betting than the horses which sometimes galloped fetlock deep in wet sand and water on Leith beach.

And thereby hangs a tale. There had been racing on the long stretch of bare sand at Leith, which was also the scene of public executions for piracy, since about 1500, probably antedating

Newmarket, York and Ayr. In 1591 George, Earl of Huntly, set off from the King's house in Edinburgh intending to stage a race meeting with about a hundred of his mounted retinue, but was distracted and crossed to Fife in order to attack the castle of Donnibristle and kill the Earl of Murray.

I suppose the defection of the entire card of runners to lay siege to a castle is among the more unusual reasons for abandonment of a race meeting, but Leith's problems were often of a more mundane nature; the difficulty was the state of the going, or more accurately, the effect of the tide.

Not only did the tide make the sand too soft and heavy for 'the generality of mettled racers', as Robert Chambers observed in his *Gazetteer of Scotland*, but it also caused contravention of the Jockey Club Rules, following the Act of Parliament, which specified that every race should begin and end on the same day; a simple enough provision to observe on the heathland of Newmarket, but not so simple when the sea surged over the course after only two heats of a three heat contest. The run-off on the following day was, strictly speaking, illegal.

It was all too much for the poor beasts, some of which literally dropped down dead in running. The quality of the sport was bound to decline, and when the exclusive if boisterous Caledonian Hunt Club withdrew their support in 1789, the writing was on the wall. This was despite the fact that those described by Chambers as 'the lower classes from the city' continued to turn up in large numbers to enjoy the racing, the revels, and the delights of the booths (temporary taverns, or beer tents) and seaside theatre, to say nothing of the attractions of the 'ladies of the town' imported for the occasion.

The pier made an excellent grandstand, and 20,000 people were reckoned to have thronged the sands in 1791, on each day of the five-day annual race week in July.

This was probably the pinnacle of Leith's success. In 1805, plans were being discussed in the *Sporting Magazine* for a turf course to be laid down at Edinburgh, with two sites on offer, as Leith races were now 'almost entirely neglected by the Scots gentry themselves . . . and no gentleman whatever from England would send horses of any value to start at Leith'.

The building of a dockyard in 1806 put the final nail into the coffin, and although racing spluttered briefly into life, at about the time that Napoleon's armies marched to defeat at Waterloo, the little Emperor and Leith races shared a similar fate.

The new racecourse was laid down on the Links of Musselburgh, an extensive plain adjacent to the ancient town, five miles from Edinburgh. The Caledonian Hunt immediately renewed its support, to the tune of a fifty-guinea donation to the poor of Musselburgh, and ten guineas to be distributed amongst the labourers who completed the course in time for the inaugural meeting of 1816, held on Monday, 7th October and lasting six days.

The Scotsman reported the victory of Lord Queensberry's Epperston in the first race, the King's Plate, of 100 guineas, a four-mile event run in three heats at 12 stone, as 'an excellent race'. The punters fared badly on the Tuesday, when Sir Alexander Don's Golumpus, the hot favourite,

LORD ROSEBERY, LEFT, AND LORD DALMENY, 1910

was beaten in a couple of two-mile heats by Mr Baillies's Jenny Rinthereout in a fifty-guinea three-year-old contest.

Sir Alexander went on a retrieval mission on the Wednesday with the money down and his brown colt by Orville won 'a severe race' in two four-mile heats; meanwhile Jenny Rinthereout ran twice more without success during the week. The darling of the crowd was Mr Michaelson's Lotta, a three-year-old who won the hundred guineas given by the Caledonian Hunt for a three-mile race on the Friday in canter for both heats, re-appearing on the Saturday to put Jenny Rinthereout firmly in her place with an easy victory in a fifty-guineas race, again sponsored by the Hunt.

By the end of a race week marked by all the social distinction of the past, the Hunt had donated three hundred guineas, the City of Edinburgh fifty guineas and there were two King's Plates of one hundred guineas each. The Marchioness of Queensberry patronised the Hunt Ball and Edmund Kean performed nightly at the theatre to packed houses; but perhaps the most significant name amongst the distinguished company was that of Lord Rosebery.

The Roseberys are steeped in racing history. The fifth Earl, who succeeded his grandfather in 1868, married the richest woman in England, Hannah, daughter of Baron Meyer de Rothschild. The Earl owned eleven classic winners, including three Derbies, and in his spare time was Prime Minister, although he found the post uncongenial, preferring to witness the Epsom victories of Ladas and Sir Visto in 1894 and '95, to the cares of office wished upon him by a Queen bored to distraction by the dullness of Gladstone.

The Rosebery family were to play a key role in the future of Edinburgh, which survived a transfer to the training grounds of Gullane in 1832 to avoid the cholera raging in the city, and the universal depression of the 'Filthy Forties'. In 1903, a group of local businessmen headed by one Robert L. Urquhart, projected plans for 'an Ascot in miniature', with grandiose designs for a new course and elaborate stands on a site to the west of the city. They took the view that 'Musselburgh does not provide everything essential to the popularity and success of present day race meetings' and the gentlemen of the consortium applied for a Jockey Club licence; but this was denied, and the venture foundered.

In 1905, the sixth Earl of Rosebery, then Lord Dalmeny, pulled off a neat double, becoming captain of the Surrey County Cricket XI and winning at Edinburgh with his first runner in Scotland, Caravel, piloted by Willie Higgs. Dalmeny was a 'fine, forcing bat' and during his captaincy of Surrey, he gave Jack Hobbs his county cap. From 1906 to 1910 he was Liberal MP for Edinburgh, thus combining, in true patrician style two activities which would be unthinkable today in a world of professional sportsmen and professional politicians.

Some may think that neither sphere is the better for that; but as Edinburgh closed for the duration of the Kaiser's War and Dalmeny joined the staff of Field-Marshal Lord Allenby, the world of sport seemed far away. Hostilities over, Musselburgh prepared to re-open in 1919, only to be thwarted by a rail strike, but racing resumed in 1920, patronised by the old friends of the Caledonian Hunt, which endowed two races each day.

Hitler caused another hiatus in 1939, the year in which the former Lord Dalmeny, now Lord Rosebery, won the Derby with Blue Peter. The Musselburgh track was again ready to admit the public in 1946, under the auspices of Alec McHarg, the Clerk of the Course, who was succeeded in 1950 by his son, Colonel William

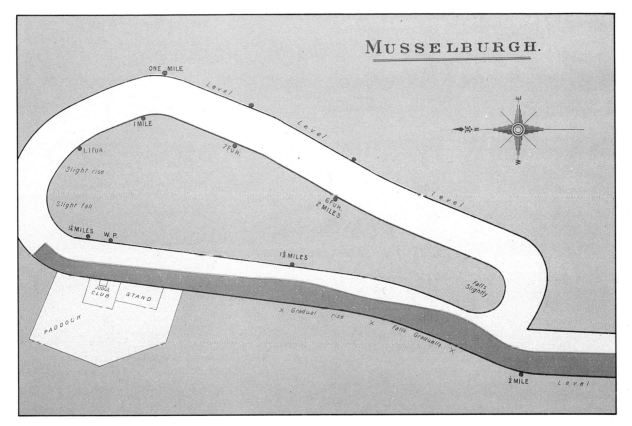

THE COURSE, 1903

McHarg, OBE, MC, TD, MA, LLB, but known to all his racing friends as Bill. Alec McHarg stayed on as joint clerk until his death in 1956.

Under the management of McHarg, Edinburgh continued in the modest but essential role of providing opportunities for moderate animals trained in Scotland and the North of England. It remained inhibited by the seaside location on common land from further development. In 1963, the Levy Board threatened to withdraw financial support, and it seemed that the historic course would have to close; but Lord Rosebery, a Steward of the Jockey Club since 1932 and twice Senior Steward, was having none of that. With all the vigour of a former forcing bat, first-class rider to hounds and polo player of international standard, together with his experience of dealing with irascible Field Marshals in the form of Lord Allenby, he told Field-Marshal Lord Harding and his Board precisely what were his opinions, and the Board relented to the extent of £700-a-day prize money added, and £2,000 towards improvements.

Incredibly, the Levy Board, by now under the chairmanship of Sir Desmond Plummer, again refused support following Rosebery's death in 1974. But by now, the old warrior's work had been well done. The opening of the Forth Road Bridge and a bridge over the River Esk made access and egress that much easier, and Musselburgh prospered; as it does today under the enterprising management of Bill McHarg's son, David, who brought National Hunt racing to the course in 1987, with great success.

So, as the Bard of Avon said, all's well that ends well; and this is merely a history, not a prognostication for the future. Even so, where will racing be in the twenty-first century if men of the kidney of Rosebery are not at hand? ■

HAMILTON

ALTHOUGH THE modern history of Hamilton dates from the mid-twenties, the beautiful Park, not unfairly described as the 'Goodwood of the North' (although the anonymous journalist presumably intended Scotland rather than the North) occupies a place deep in the history of Scotland and England.

The park is enclosed on an estate which originally formed part of the royal forest of Cadzow, where King David I of Scotland hunted the wild white Caledonian bull from his seat at Cadzow Castle around 1130. A hundred years later, as the feudal system was being established in Scotland under King Alexander II, then married to Joan, daughter of King John of England, some land was granted to Sir Gilbert de Hamilton, whose family, the de Bellomonts, were among the Conqueror's entourage of 1066.

Gilbert's son Walter acted as bodyguard to Robert the Bruce at the Battle of Bannockburn, and for loyal service was rewarded with the barony of Cadzow, thus founding the great Scottish house of Hamilton.

Three centuries later, James, third Marquis of Hamilton, played a significant role in Charles I's tussle with the Scottish Covenanters and the King created him Duke of Hamilton in 1643, with the unusual provision of a matriarchal law of inheritance. The device proved to be useful, as both Hamilton and his brother were to die in the service of the King, James losing his head on the execution block and brother William receiving fatal wounds at the battle of Worcester, leaving James's daughter Anne to continue the line.

A period of mixed fortunes, during which one Duke was killed in a duel in Hyde Park and a successor married the celebrated beauty Elizabeth Gunning, preceded the inaugural race meeting at Hamilton Park, in the shadow of the magnificent ducal palace.

It was Tuesday, 6th August, 1782. The Duke of Hamilton's Disguise was an appropriate winner of the first event, for a purse of fifty guineas and run in two four-mile heats.

The next day saw a Ladies' Purse, again of fifty guineas, for all ages and incorporating the interesting condition that three-year-olds should carry a feather; a feather being a boy rider who was so light that he was not called upon to either weigh in or out. Again, the winning owner was the Duke of Hamilton.

The Duke's monopoly continued the following year and was still in evidence when the meeting was extended to three days in 1785. Understandably, rival owners found this somewhat dispiriting, and the fixture was scrapped after only three horses turned up to contest a two-day card in 1793.

The Caledonian Hunt Club attempted a revival in 1800 with an ambitious five-day meeting, but again there was a paucity of runners, and after four events had resulted in walk-overs the following year, the Hunt were reduced to staging donkey races, a regular diversion of the period. Perhaps it would have been even more diverting if they had revived an event run at London's Tothill Fields in 1791 when 'Six jackasses started for a gold laced hat, which was won by half a neck. Three young ladies ran for a holland smock in their shifts and under petticoats'.

Little more was heard of Hamilton for over

A PARK RANGER.

STARTING POST FOR THE MILE.
(OPPOSITE THE PALACE.)

THE STRAIGHT COURSE, FROM
THE TRAINERS' STAND.

G.D.A.

HAMILTON PARK

Hamilton Park

eighty years, until a group of whisky magnates approached one of their more valued customers, Sir John Astley, known to all as The Mate, with a view to persuading Sir John to design a course and act as first Clerk. The Mate knew a lot about racing, but little about administration, being more concerned with the broader side of life. A former Member of Parliament, he was heckled during a campaign speech and asked by an earnest seeker after knowledge for an opinion on Sir Wilfrid Lawson's Liquor Bill. Astley had never heard of either Lawson or the Bill, but replied smartly: 'I don't know much about Sir Wilfrid Lawson's Liquor Bill, but I know that mine is a deuced sight too high this year!'

Encountering a well-endowed lady in a tightly-fitting dress in the paddock at Newmarket, Sir John observed, 'Ah, Form at a Glance, I suppose.' He was not an ideal choice for the new venture, but he probably needed the money as usual, and although taking the gloomy view that the Scots didn't really care for horse racing, went ahead and the new course, still within the confines of the park, opened on 12th July, 1888 with a two-day programme.

George Barrett rode the first winner, Wild West II, trained by Bob Armstrong at Penrith. Prize money was poor, the fixture never became properly established, and not even the skills of Sir Loftus Bates, the John Hughes of his day, who became Clerk in 1897, could save it. To the disappointment of the steeplechasing fraternity who found the winter gatherings an agreeable way of passing the time, even if the runners did outnumber the spectators, Hamilton folded again

in 1907. This doubtless had the blessing of the Duchess of Hamilton, who was reluctant to renew the lease as she considered that gambling was bad for the working classes.

But the intrepid Sir Loftus was not done with yet. The Edwardian era passed into the conflict of Mons, Verdun and Passchendaele and emerged into the frantic fun-seeking twenties. The time seemed ripe for another attempt, and together with Lord Hamilton of Dalzell and Col. Thomas Robertson-Aikman, a new £100,000 company was formed.

Although some of the Glaswegian fun-seekers preferred the urban delights of greyhound racing, forty thousand punters patronised the opening of the new course, looped in the manner of Salisbury and laid out on higher ground away from the old track on the banks of the Clyde.

The date was 16th July, 1926. Bob Armstrong, who had triumphed in the inaugural race on the old course back in 1888, again trained the winner of the first, the Cambusnethan Handicap Plate over a mile. Joe Thwaites steered Impress home at 9/2 and went on to complete a double in the next, a seller, on Fritters, winning by a short head at the rewarding odds of 100/7.

Success came slowly. Runners were still thin on the ground – even the Hamilton Inaugural Cup on 17th July was followed by a walk-over for the Cambusland Two-Year-Old Plate. Scottish trainers unsympathetically preferred to run their horses on the richer-picking fields of England, while, ironically, Yorkshire trainers were happy to race in Scotland and provided the backbone of the sport. A boost came in the form of a royal visit by

30

Hamilton Park

SIR LOFTUS BATES AND MORAG CHALMERS

Their Majesties King George V and Queen Mary, and Hamilton settled down to an existence best described as pastoral.

In 1947, Sir Loftus was succeeded by W.H. Robertson-Aikman, whose family connection with Hamilton dated back to the days of the Covenanters in 1679. The new Clerk instigated the first night racing in the British Isles on 18th July 1947, with a card commencing at 6 p.m. and a crowd of 18,000 in attendance. Major John Fairfax-Blakeborough does, however, mention, in his *Northern Turf History*, a report of racing at York in 1784 where the fifth race was run in the dark, and in a remarkably fast time; doubtless the jockeys cut a few corners.

In 1971, Hamilton became the first course to race on a Saturday morning, an experiment which has had decidedly less impact than the evening idea. Today, Hamilton is prospering under the management of David McHarg and has recently recorded another first, when Miss Morag Chalmers became Clerk of the Course; a happy combination for one of the prettiest courses in Britain. ∎

BEVERLEY

WHAT USED to be the East Riding of Yorkshire is now known as Humberside and here lies the ancient town of Beverley which boasts two of the most beautiful churches in England, and has been a centre of country sports for many centuries.

Racing at Westwood and Hurn meadows certainly took place in 1690, and by 1734 was well established with the usual cock-fighting amusing the punters after racing, the battles being fought between the birds of Beverley and Hull. In 1767 a grandstand was erected at a cost of over a thousand pounds, raised by the issue of three hundred and thirty silver life members' badges.

Although they are thin on the ground today, there is quite a history of men of the cloth taking to the Turf as owners and breeders, even of classic winners; in 1874, John Porter trained Apology to win the Oaks and the St Leger for 'Mr Launde', the nom-de-course of the Rev. Mr King.

Perhaps the best known cleric to grace the Turf was the Rev. Henry Goodricke, owner of at least four St Leger winners, usually carrying the pink and black colours of his close friend Mr Gilbert Crompton. Known as a man who could outlast most three-bottle squires after dinner, Goodricke's runners went through the card at the Beverley meeting in 1800. Today it would be interesting to have the reverend gentleman's view on Sunday racing.

As the home of the Holderness Hunt, the reputation of Beverley rose while York races suffered a period of decline in the mid-nineteenth century. Beverley race week was sullied only by a barbarous football match played through the streets of the town annually on the Sunday before racing between the 'lads' of Beverley and a team representing the surrounding villages. Standing no nonsense, the town fathers put a stop to the yearly mayhem by sending the Mayor at the head of forty militiamen to read the Riot Act, which was received by the hooligans with jeers and chants. The soldiers then charged with fixed bayonets, and the wretched rabble dispersed, never to return.

The Holderness Hunt staged National Hunt races on the course between 1828 and 1839 and by now Beverley was well established as a training centre. From his stud and stables at nearby Bishop Burton, Squire Richard Watt sent out four St Leger winners, Altisidora (1813), Barefoot (1823), Memnon (1825) and Rockingham (1833). Altisidora is commemorated by the name of a pub in Bishop Burton, and the Watt Memorial Stakes at the June meeting perpetuates the memory of Squire Watt. But the true heroine of the period was the locally bred filly Nancy, winner of the Ebor, the Goodwood Cup and conqueror of the great Voltigeur in the York and Ainsty Cup at York, albeit in a race run at a funereal pace. Her victory in the Chester Cup of 1851 with a featherweight 4st 12lb broke the bookies' hearts as her Yorkshire supporters backed her off the boards.

The winner by a neck from Black Doctor, Nancy then spent thirteen hours in a horsebox to Scotland before winning Lord Glasgow's Three Hundred Sovereigns Plate. Poor Nancy was later killed when she broke a leg at Chester.

Job Marson Snr trained Nancy, and his son Job Jnr rode Voltigeur and six classic winners in all, proving that Beverley could breed top jockeys as well as top horses. Len Jewison and John Cade were star knights of the pigskin in the eighteenth century, and the alcoholic but brilliant Jim Snowden partnered Blair Athol to win the Derby and Leger of 1864. He also rode Butterfly (1860) and Jenny Howlett (1880) to victory in the Oaks. Apprenticed at Beverley, Snowden died in poverty in 1889 and lies beneath a memorial in nearby Pocklington churchyard subscribed by his many racing friends.

The course at Westwood is rented by the Race Company from the pasture-masters, who acquired the land by virtue of a payment of one hundred shillings to Archbishop Neville of York in 1380. As at Epsom and other courses where racing takes place on common ground, the requirements of the local community and those of the racing fraternity have not always been in accord.

Things came to a head in 1902 when the Race Company were seeking a new site for the sports and the pasture-masters were wondering how much more money there was in sheep.

Presumably not a lot. By 1903, F.H. Bayles was able to report that all the various ploys had fallen through on both sides and that racing would continue on the 'good old turf' which was based on a deep subsoil of alluvium, with a substratum of chalk, producing very soft going in wet weather, unlike most chalk-based tracks.

The three-day June meeting of the 1840s had been reduced to a two-day affair. Bayles described the event as having 'little interest outside its own districts, and that of the northern trainers; this may be due to the smallness of the stakes, which are insufficient to attract the patronage of the southern stables, which form the keystone of all successful race meetings. There are no races here with added money of more than £200 and but few of these. Unless, therefore, the Executive is sufficiently prudent and enterprising to offer larger inducements, I am afraid that Beverley will never acquire the support of these indispensable stables'.

Bayles was right and when Colonel Sidney Renton took over control of the Race Company just after the war, things were much as they had been in Bayles's day, with only two day's sport in the *Calendar*. Under Renton's enterprising management, a new Members' Stand was built in 1949, and by 1965 seven days' racing was on the cards. A £112,000 Levy Board grant provided a new Tatt's in 1967, and an aggressive sponsorship programme has produced a card of eighteen days a year.

Today, two races in particular stir the memories of bygone years. The humble Kiplingcotes Selling Stakes remembers one of the oldest races in the world, run first in 1619 with conditions stipulating that 'Every rider that layeth hold of any of the other riders, or striketh any of them, shall win no prize!'. The four-mile course was from Etton to Middleton-on-the-Wolds, and was to lapse forever if not contested every year. Horses were walked round the course in the bitter winter of 1947 when weather conditions prevented the race, and the Kiplingcotes or 'Kippleing Coates' in the original spelling, is still run today, although not under Jockey Club Rules.

The Bishop Burton Stakes is now a five-furlong sprint for older horses, but in 1865 it was a two-year-old event and won by Blink Bonny as one of her eight juvenile victories, including the Gimcrack. She went on to win the Derby and the Oaks,

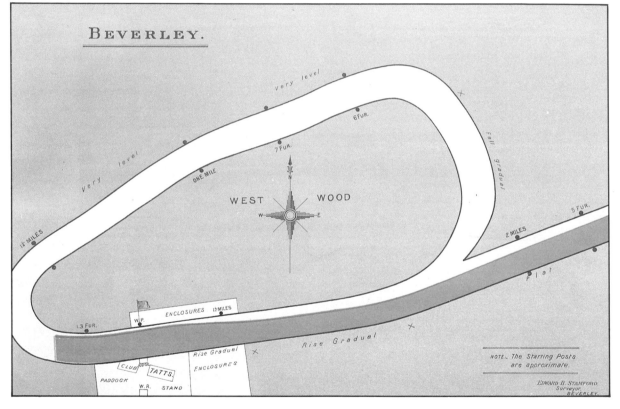

THE COURSE, 1903

and would have won the St Leger but for being pulled by her jockey, John Charlton, at the behest of a bookmaker.

One of only four fillies to win both of the Epsom classics, Blink Bonny represents the golden days of northern racing and training: an epoch which seems unlikely to return in the eyes of posterity, although posterity is as likely to be wrong as anybody else. ∎

CARLISLE

I T IS hard to imagine the seventh-century Norseman, bearded and rugged beneath his horned helmet, salt-stained from his longboat and dedicated to rape and pillage, as a racing buff. However, the Cumberland historian Walter McIntyre is of the opinion that the earliest form of racing at Carlisle was under the auspices of sporting festivals organised by the invaders on the land much later known as Kingsmoor.

It was called Kynges Moor in the reign of James I when, in 1619, racing was revived after languishing in late Elizabethan times. This was despite the presentation in 1559 of one of racing's oldest surviving trophies, the Gold Bell, donated by Lady Dacre, wife of the Governor of the City.

The races had fallen into disrepute as victim of that old enemy, crowd violence, common enough at the time and recorded at Doncaster races in 1615, when the meeting had to be prohibited by city ordinance. Gang warfare was probably the problem at Carlisle, with one William Armstrong, known to terrorists and terrified alike as 'Kinmont Willie' strutting the course with his attendant thugs to settle some bloody local feuds.

The revival was a definite success and it was intended by the Mayor 'and his bretheren', by public demand, that the races should continue 'at such tyme yearley as they shall think convenient'. It is likely that Lady Dacre's Gold Bell, charmingly inscribed 'The Sweftes Horse This Bel to Tak For Mi Lade Daker Sake', was competed for until the Commonwealth. A smaller bell was given by Henry Baines, Mayor of Carlisle, or Karliell in contemporary spelling, and was also raced for during the period.

THE CARLISLE BELL

Possibly, racing resumed on Kingsmoor in the heady days of the Restoration as the people relaxed and amused themselves with all the customary Cumberland sports including hound trailing, hawking, bowling and archery, but the next recorded activity is at a new venue, the Swifts, shown as a racecourse on a local map of 1746.

Two meetings, one a four-day event, were listed in the *Calendar* of 1773 and the King's Plate was a two-hundred guinea race in 1792 at the October meeting, but by 1839 this was reduced to one hundred guineas and the meetings were down to one three-day gathering in late October.

The signs were ominous, and few courses were to escape the evils of the 'Filthy Forties'. The great days when the gentry in their carriages lined the course to the distance pole, with hundreds more spectators mounted and on foot, to see the likes of local hero Springkell win the Gold Cups of 1825, '27 and '28, were fading when another equine favourite, Lanercost, triumphed at 5/1 on in 1840.

Springkell was actually a raider from the South of Scotland, bred by his owner Sir John Maxwell and named after Maxwell's seat near Ecclefechan. Springkell also won the King's Plate at Carlisle in 1827 and was a standing dish at his home course of Dumfries during his four-year career, sporting a Scottish fan club that made regular excursions southward to follow his exploits at Carlisle and Newcastle.

Lanercost had a much more varied career, finishing third to Don John in the St Leger in 1838. Bred in Cumberland and originally trained in Yorkshire, Lanercost was sent as a four-year-old to William I'Anson at Gullane in East Lothian, from whence he travelled the 340-mile journey to Newmarket in a tiny three-wheeled horse box to win the inaugural Cambridgeshire in the hands of William Noble in 1839.

Two minor St Leger winners, Warlock and Caller Ou went pot-hunting on the Swifts in the 1860s, but otherwise there was little to cheer about as attendances dwindled and trainers took their horses elsewhere, only thirty-one runners mustering for the 1864 meeting.

Things improved a little as the railway network spread its way across northern England in the late nineteenth century, bringing with it an abundance of company names; the Maryport and Carlisle, the Midland and the London and North Western all competed to convey punters and runners to Carlisle, and a grandstand was erected for the first time.

It was all to no avail. In 1904 the lease held on the Swifts from the Duke of Devonshire expired, and His Grace decided not to grant a further term.

This was considered by some to be a blessing in disguise. The Swifts was on the bank of the River Eden and in addition to frequent flooding, the tight turn for home sent many an unhappy nag slithering into the water.

A new site was found at a farm south of Carlisle called Blackwell and a course was financed by a newly formed Race Company, who perhaps knew more about racing than public relations or transportation. Road access was poor, and the nearest station was in the city or two miles away at Cummersdale, even though the London and North Western line bordered the course.

Not surprisingly, the project failed, and the property seemed likely to return to agricultural use when the hour produced the man. Sir Loftus Bates, Brigadier-General, D.S.O., former trainer and at various times Clerk of the Course at Hamilton Park, Kelso, Hexham, Perth, Thirsk, Pontefract and Catterick knew a bit about the administration of racing. The ex-Dragoon Guards officer lost no time in forming a fresh Race Company, smartening up the stands, re-designing the course and persuading the local council to widen the access road.

Carlisle

The London and North Western agreed to a Halt and a race-train service. Sir Loftus continued to preside over a now thriving track until handing over to C.D. 'Kit' Patterson in 1946. Sir Loftus died in 1951, shortly after relinquishing the Managing Directorship of Kelso, and his contribution to northern and Scottish racing in a career of administration spanning fifty-four years cannot be measured.

THE OLD TOTE BAR

Typically, he was one of the original minds behind the introduction of the Tote on British racecourses, together with the Brigadier-General's great friend, Lord Hamilton of Dalzell; and Carlisle nearly made Turf history on 2nd July, 1929 by declaring the first dividend. Sadly for the Cumberland course, Newmarket ran a race fifteen minutes earlier.

It was, needless to say, the same gallant officer who restored the Carlisle Bells which had been found in the office of the Town Clerk in the late nineteenth century after vanishing about two hundred years earlier. In 1922, the Bells were kept in the local museum, and Sir Loftus decided to found the Carlisle Bell Handicap, the winning owner to receive a replica of Lady Dacre's original trophy.

The Carlisle Bell and the historic Cumberland Plate are the principal races run today, both at the main meeting in late June or early July.

Despite the nearby industrial conurbation surrounding the ancient city, the lakeland setting is attractive with the hills forming a background to the admittedly modest contests which are nonetheless enjoyed by the knowledgeable northern crowds who find easy access from the adjacent M6 motorway. ■

CATTERICK

CATTERICK IS about five miles south-east of the historic and beautiful town of Richmond, in the old North Riding of Yorkshire. Both townships stand on the River Swale, and a mile to the north of Catterick the Swale is crossed by a bridge, on which was formerly a chapel. Opposite lies the racecourse which took its name from Catterick Bridge when the first recorded meeting took place on 22nd April, 1783.

Catterick was founded more in a spirit of sport than with any thoughts of commercialism. For over a century admission was free, the races were either for private side-stakes or for prizes in kind, usually of an alcoholic nature, and the executive incurred little cost apart from the tar and feathers required for welshing bookmakers.

Much of this cheerful Corinthian spirit could doubtless be found at the George and Dragon Inn and posting house nearby, where mine host was Tom Ferguson, owner of the controversial St Leger winner, Antonio, in 1819. Antonio had made his first appearance in the Old Stakes at Catterick on 15th April, well beaten in a two-horse race, and was little fancied for the Leger, which he won after several strong contenders had been left. The Doncaster stewards ordered a re-run, in which Antonio did not take part, but the Jockey Club later called the second 'race' void, and awarded the stakes to Antonio. The colt was promptly sold by Ferguson, who knew how lucky he was to win with such a moderate animal.

The shrewd publican was right, and Antonio proved to be of no further account either on the racecourse or at stud. Apart from the George and Dragon and the posting business, Ferguson, al-though a breeder of bloodstock, was primarily a breeder of coach horses and kept anything up to fifty horses at Catterick.

He also thought nothing of driving a flock of sheep on endless circuits of the sharp little track, only just over a mile round, to clear an unseasonal fall of snow and make racing possible when abandonment seemed certain. But this happy state of inspired improvisation could not last for ever, as racing became more professional and the Jockey Club imposed mandatory levels of prize money.

Given the catchment area of Catterick in the mid-nineteenth century, it was not easy to increase either public or financial support, but it was not for want of trying, and in the 1840's the two-day meeting in Easter week boasted a two-year-old sweepstake of twenty sovereigns each, over a mile, and the Claret Stakes, of eighteen sovereigns each, with fifteen added from the club fund. This event for older horses over two miles included the proviso, not uncommon at the time, that the winner should give two guineas to John Orton, the judge.

On the second day, the six-furlong Champagne Stakes for juveniles was another twenty sovereign stakes race with fifteen added, less the two guineas for Mr Orton, and the main feature was a Gold Cup, or specie (cash) at the option of the winner; the stakes were ten sovereigns and the distance three miles.

All this compared well enough with Richmond, then racing on Whitcliffe pasture, Beverley and Ripon, although Ripon did put up a £100 Gold Cup. But the appeal remained strictly localised, as F.H. Bayles confirmed in 1903.

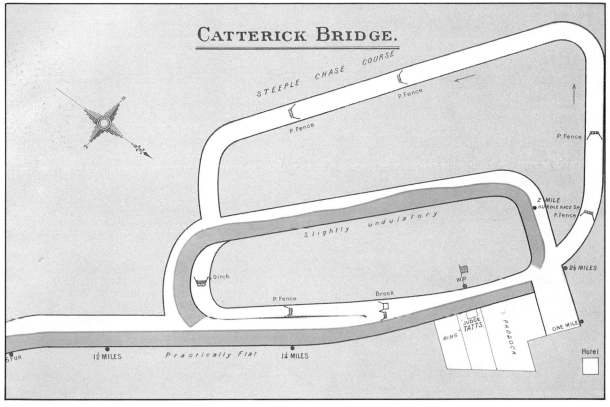

THE COURSE, 1903

'The Catterick Bridge Meeting, which is held in April for two days, is but little patronised by southerners. Yet its meed of influence and patronage amongst the sportsmen and gentry in the North Riding of Yorkshire is liberally bestowed, while the races are particularly attractive locally.'

At this time there was no grandstand, and neither six- nor seven-furlong courses. The track curved sharply at both ends of the oval, almost rectangular-shaped, 'round' course and mile races started behind the paddock wall, the field having to negotiate a ninety-degree left-hand turn before 'intercepting', as Bayles put it, a very nice gallop for just under three furlongs before another virtual right-angle brought them towards the home straight. Then, as now, the five-furlong course started with a steep downhill descent and was one of the fastest in the country.

A stand was built in 1906, and a Race Com-

pany formed in 1923, but Catterick remained in the doldrums, alleviated only by the odd incident such as that recounted by Jack Leach; in fact Jack thought it was such a good story that he told it in both volumes of his reminiscences, 'Sods I Have Cut on the Turf' and 'A Rider on the Stand'. This is how it goes:

One day in the twenties, Leach was riding a short runner (i.e. a horse which does not truly stay five furlongs) at Catterick called Garter Queen. Generally, this type of animal requires patient handling, being waited with to save the little amount of stamina and make the speed tell at the finish.

However, the jockey reasoned that on the sharp 'five' at Catterick, if he broke fast he could poach an unassailable lead. The plan worked, Garter Queen duly 'pinged' out of the old barrier starting gate, and at half-way was a good twelve

LESLIE PETCH

lengths up on her rivals.

A furlong from home, inevitably, she began to stop, and was soon beaten as Harry Wragg and Davie McGuigan shot past, locked in battle, and Tommy Weston's mount pipped Garter Queen on the line for third. As they trotted back, Leach looked into the 'frame' beside the judge's box and was astounded to see his number on top. Wragg and McGuigan were arguing as to which of them had won, and Leach took some pleasure in telling them that he had, to their mutual chagrin.

Of course, Garter Queen hadn't won, but Leach's theory that he was so far in front with a furlong to go that the judge had decided that Garter Queen must win and concentrated on the others in the finish, is plausible and the result was not amended. Leach kept the race, although he reckons he was beaten at least one and a half lengths.

In 1946, Major Leslie Petch became Clerk of the Course. The man who was to revive the fortunes of Redcar and who made York one of the finest courses in Europe, lost no time in grappling with difficult financial problems, re-designing the track and improving the standards for both horse and human. As at York, he was succeeded in this task by his nephew John Sanderson and although the quality of the racing is not high, today Catterick is an important minor venue for northern trainers and racegoing public alike.

Practical rather than picturesque, the course now stages fourteen days' racing a year and, if snow falls for the April meeting, all the Clerk of the Course will need is a little of the Tom Ferguson sporting spirit and a few co-operative sheep. ■

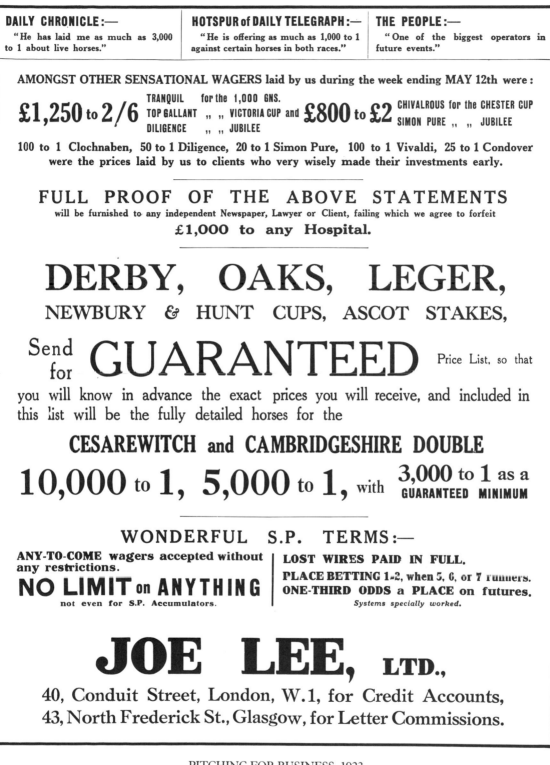

PITCHING FOR BUSINESS, 1923

DONCASTER

'*The fittest horse wins the Two Thousand Guineas, the luckiest horse wins the Derby, but the best horse wins the St Leger.*' – Old Turf proverb.

'*Winter follows close on the tail of the last horse at the Doncaster St Leger meeting.*' – Old Yorkshire saying.

To THE Roman legions it was known as the Danum of Antoninus; the Saxons called it Dona Ceastre and it was the residence of the Kings of Northumbria. Racing probably took place on Town Moor, Doncaster, before 1600, and racing was certainly intended there in 1615 before being prohibited by the Mayor and Corporation on the grounds of 'quarrels, murders and bloodsheds that may ensue by the continuing of the said races', a decision which doesn't say a lot for the conduct of the early seventeenth-century racegoer.

However, the ban was short-lived and the following year the Corporation were happy to receive twelve pence to provide a right of way for racehorses 'at the water gap'. The next recorded meeting, as advertised in the *London Gazette*, took place on 23rd July, 1684, and by 1703, the Corporation were astonished to discover that they had been contributing five pounds a year to a race plate without their knowledge, as the Mayor had tactfully omitted to tell his Council colleagues when authorising the grant.

The Corporation gracefully accepted the *fait accompli* and felt it their duty to continue to support the local meeting, but reduced the contribution to four guineas, and this somewhat parsimonious gesture began an association with Doncaster Races which has lasted to this day.

There are no records of the races as run until 1728, when a three-day meeting commenced on 22nd July. Three races, one each day, were contested in four-mile heats by a total of fourteen horses for an aggregate purse of £73.

The first-known Doncaster winner was Drummer, owned by Captain the Hon. Hugh Collyer. The next went to Lord Gower's Trentham and the give-and-take (handicap race) was won by Mr Clapham's wonderfully named Sweetest-when-naked.

The meeting moved to August in 1729, but both prize money and fields were poor. An injection of cash failed to win much more support, and neither did a decision in 1731 to hold the races in the first week in June. Other dates were tried, including May and October, but it was September that proved the most successful, and by 1751 was proving to be a social success as well.

In that year, 4,000 mounted noblemen, squires and yeomen met the Marquis of Granby's Staghounds on the Town Moor for a spot of hunting in the morning, followed by an afternoon's racing, on each day of the meeting. Lord Granby had married Lady Frances Seymour in 1750, and the hounds were part of her dowry. Normally kennelled at Newmarket, the pack provided extra amusement for the Doncaster sportsmen already enjoying hare coursing, cub hunting and cock-fighting as part of the race week carnival.

1751 also saw the inauguration of the Race Week Ball, held at the recently refurbished Mansion House and inspired by a similar event which

Doncaster

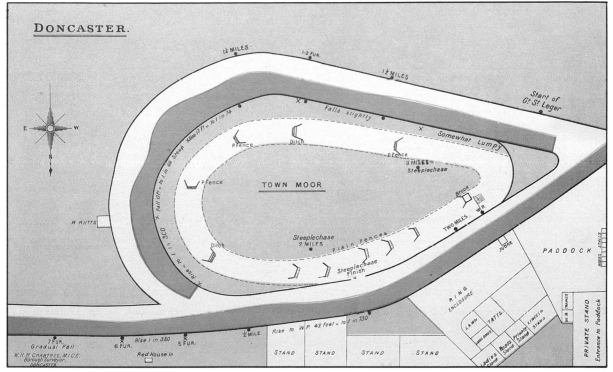

THE COURSE, 1903

ANTHONY ST LEGER

had proved popular at York's August meeting. All the Yorkshire county families were there, led by the Marquis of Rockingham and his guests, the Italian Princes Mark and Baptist Borghese. There were also some elegant young ladies present, several doubtless anxious to catch the eligible Princes' eyes; so many in fact that the *York Courant* reporter was forced to describe one family collectively as 'the Misses Yarborough (4)'.

In 1752, with the Corporation firmly in charge, a four-day meeting was staged and the Marquis of Rockingham donated a fifty-guinea plate to be run in three two-mile heats for horses which had never won a £50 race. Not surprisingly, this event attracted the largest field ever known at Doncaster, and twelve horses took part.

The winner was Mr Bowes's Cato, but of far greater significance was the interest of Lord Rockingham. This future Prime Minister, who formed Whig governments in 1765 and 1782, was already a prominent member of the York Race Executive and seemed determined to make Town Moor equal the success of the Knavesmire. To this end, Rockingham fleshed out sparse Doncaster programmes with match races arranged with his aristocratic friends during various country house parties. At the same time he bullied the Corporation into providing financial assistance and acknowledging the importance of the races to the town.

As ever, the civic dignitaries were reluctant to part with the ratepayers' cash to subsidise such a trivial pastime as the Turf, but Rockingham's pressure brought an £80 Gold Cup, considered essential at the time for any meeting wishing to be regarded as first-class. Thus, in 1766, the first Doncaster Cup was run in three four-mile heats, with five-year-olds carrying 7st 10lb, six-year-olds weighted at 8st 7lb, aged horses at 9st. The winner was Lord Archibald Hamilton's chestnut mare Charlotte.

In Volume III of the late Major John Fairfax-Blakeborough's invaluable and absorbing *Northern* Turf History, he gives the following balance sheet for the 1775 season, prepared by Thomas Stannell, the Corporation's accountant and Clerk of the Course. Stannell's own fee was ten guineas. Other disbursements included a guinea to the man who sounded the alarm when the races were 'off', three guineas to be shared among the Town Waites (singers) and five guineas for the three 'musitions'. Lord Scarborough's French-horn man was paid four guineas, which shows that it paid to work for the aristocracy in the eighteenth century.

Two men and a horse for clearing the course received a mere 15 shillings; advertising in 'the London papers' came to £1. 7s. od, and the intriguing item 'running over Johnson's flat' cost half-a-crown. Who was Johnson, and what took place in his flat? It was presumably a piece of land requiring payment for right of way.

Nonetheless, a reasonable profit was shown with a total income of £311. 18s. 6d, including donations of ten guineas each from the Lords Rockingham and Scarborough and £50 from the Corporation.

Meanwhile, in his mansion at nearby Park Hill, Colonel Anthony St Leger was seeking inspiration. St Leger, whose name is properly pronounced Sellinger, was born in Ireland in 1732

THE RED LION HOTEL

and became a successful soldier and later Governor of St Lucia. A keen racing man, farmer and patron of the theatre, St Leger had become interested in races confined to three-year-olds, the first of which had been run over two miles on the Beacon Course at Newmarket on 4th October, 1756.

St Leger decided that three was the perfect testing age for the thoroughbred, and races confined to that age usually produced competitive fields. Accordingly, he devised a two-mile race for colts and fillies, a sweepstakes of 25 guineas each, colts to carry 8st and fillies 7st 12lb.

A field of six faced the starter on 24th September, 1776 for what was to be the world's first classic race. It was not on Town Moor, but at the adjacent Cantley Common, and it was probably no surprise that the winner was Lord Rockingham's filly by Sampson, although it might have been, as the *Calendar* records the betting as '2/1 on Lord Rockingham's *colt*'!

None of the horses in the race was named; Col. St Leger (described in the racecard as Mr St Leger, which must have pleased him) ran a brown filly by Trusty, finishing second, and another well-known local sportsman, Mr Peregrine Wentworth, owned the third, a bay colt by Doge.

The jockeys are not listed in the *Calendar*, but we know that the winning rider was John Singleton, not to be confused with his son of the same name also a successful jockey. After his victory on the Sampson filly, Singleton Snr went to France and trained for the Duc d'Orléans, sensibly leaving France before the revolution to run a pub near York racecourse. He rode his last winner at Chester in 1784 and died in poverty at the age of ninety-four in Chester Workhouse. He is reputed to have ridden Eclipse in many of his races, but there is no evidence of this.

So, an unnamed horse won an unnamed race, but not for long; Lord Rockingham eventually named them both. The Sampson filly was later called Allabaculia according to John Orton's *Turf Annals* of 1844, although Allabaculia's name does not appear in either the *Calendar* for 1777 or the *Stud Book*. Nonetheless, Allabaculia is regarded as being the name of the winner, and as to the name of the race, there can be no doubt.

As was the invariable custom in these matters, the name was decided at a dinner party. Lord Derby.'s famous post-prandial session at the Oaks in 1779 to christen the Derby may have stolen a bit of Yorkshire thunder over the years, but the gathering hosted by Lord Rockingham after John Cade had piloted Bourbon to victory in the second running of the still unnamed race, is of equal importance.

There is some doubt over the venue; it is generally accepted that the party, attended by 'the Mayor, the Corporation, officials and some distinguished owners and supporters', took place at the Red Lion Hotel in Doncaster after racing, and given the presence of the civic worthies, this seems likely.

However, the distinguished journalist, Scarth Dixon, records a dinner party hosted by Rockingham at the Marquis's seat at Wentworth Woodhouse in 1777 and recites a guest list which does not include Mayor, Corporation or officials, at least not as such. Col. St Leger was amongst the gentlemen present, assembled in order to discuss their nominations for the 1778 race, and it is quite possible that this was the occasion when Rockingham declined the proposal that the race should be named in his honour, saying, 'No, it was my friend St Leger who suggested the thing to me –

call it after him'. And so it was.

The Wentworth party seems to be much more Rockingham's style and I think that is probably what happened; but, as Noel Coward said of the disputed works of Shakespeare, 'What does it matter – the sonnets were written', and the St Leger was named. It was, of course, known as the Sellinger Stakes for many years while the Doncaster meeting was still dominated by the local gentry who knew the correct pronunciation of St Leger's name.

The dashing Colonel was known as something of a ladies' man. As a guest at the Duke of Richmond's table when the latter was Lord Lieutenant of Ireland, and St Leger was on the Duke's staff, with the gallant, if eccentric manners of the period, he drank the contents of the Duchess's finger bowl after she had dipped her digits following the dessert. The Duke crustily observed, 'I say, Sellinger, Her Grace washes her feet at night; would you like to have that?'

In 1778, the first St Leger to bear the name was moved from the original site at Cantley Common, hard by Carr House and Cantley Hall, where, in 1714, Leonard Childers had bred Flying Childers, 'The Fleetest Horse in Britain'. It moved to Town Moor, home of the Leger ever since, excepting wartime substitute races.

Stands were built by the York racecourse architect John Carr at a cost of £2,637; other improvements cost £7,282. 17s. A silver perpetual members badge was seven guineas, and the race went to Hollandaise, owned by Sir Thomas Gascoigne (a guest at the Wentworth dinner party) and ridden by George Herring. Herring's riding

THE POT HOUSE

THE GRAND STAND

DONCASTER IN 1874

SALUTATION

THE SALUTATION

THE ST. LÉGER MEETING

THE ROOMS

DOWN THE AVENUE

exploits are reputed to have included nineteen consecutive winners, which, if true, make Gordon Richards' 1933 record of twelve seem pretty small beer, but the habit of omitting jockeys' names from the *Calendar* makes verification impossible.

Conditions for the early St Legers were a little odd by modern standards. Horses in those days had to walk to the races, and animals entered for the race had to be 'shown' at a spot outside the town called Lousy Bush Close.

The race did not achieve national importance until Frank Buckle rode local Doncaster owner Christopher Wilson's Epsom hero, Champion, to complete the first Derby-St Leger double in 1800. However, the St Leger swiftly gained the reputation of the North's premier race. The weights were changed in 1790, colts to carry 8st 2lb and fillies 7st 12lb, but that did not deter the first St Leger specialist, John Mangle, from recording his fifth win on Tartar in 1792. Mangle, known as 'Crying Jackie' because of his habit of bursting into tears when the result of a close race went against him, would have made it six but for being disqualified for 'jostling' on Zanga, first past the post in 1789. How this setback affected him emotionally is not known, but Mangle's Leger record included a hat-trick of victories in 1786, 1787 and 1788.

In 1793 the race was won, appropriately enough, by Ninety-Three, ridden by William Pierse, a jockey who had shown his early promise riding in private matches while employed as a postillion by Lady Mary Carr, sister of the Earl of Darlington. These races were at catch-weights, and as Pierse weighed out at 3st 7lb, his victories in the matches were as unsurprising as his original

career playing Tom Thumb in pantomime and his subsequent career as a top-flight rider.

The Town Moor crowds of 1795 were privileged to witness the St Leger victory of one of the great Northern champions, Hambletonian, a grandson of Eclipse. The day after the Leger, Hambletonian won the Doncaster Cup, and won the Cup again in 1796, beating that year's Leger winner, Ambrosio. Perhaps his finest hour was not on Town Moor, but at Newmarket in 1799 when, ridden by Frank Buckle, he beat Diamond with Dennis Fitzpatrick up, in a 3,000 guinea match over four miles and one furlong of the Beacon course. Hambletonian gave Diamond three pounds and started at 5/4 on in front of a huge crowd of Yorkshiremen who had travelled to cheer their champion home.

By the turn of the century, the St Leger was becoming a national event. Balls and houseparties for the gentry became a well-established custom and every hostelry in Doncaster overflowed in every sense during race week. The tradition of the eve of St Leger dinner goes back to 1803, when it was ordered by the Corporation that 'the Mayor shall hire the fat cook at the Angel, called Winterbotham, to cook at the Mansion House, upon the same terms as the other two women kept there, and paid by the Corporation at 17/6d for the week'.

In the same year, Joseph Lockwood became Clerk of the Course, also officiating as starter and judge. He remained in office until succeeded by his son, Joseph Jnr, in 1831. Although Lockwood Snr was not always an unqualified success as either starter or judge, these offices were not easy options in the early nineteenth century, and in general

FLYING CHILDERS

terms he presided over a prosperous period of Doncaster's history.

Also in 1803, a King's Plate of 100 guineas was transferred from Burford when that meeting became extinct. The Plate had originated with Charles II at Newmarket, but when the Merry Monarch had a little bother with Parliament in 1681, he dissolved the assembly and told them to meet at Oxford in March. Not wishing to miss the races for the Plate, he transferred the Newmarket meeting as well, to the Cotswold town of Burford, and while the politicians seethed, the King and his son, the Duke of Monmouth, took part in the races.

Unhappily, the first running of the King's Plate at Doncaster was a walk-over for Stockton, owned by Colonel Henry Mellish. This gallant officer typified his period, and the description 'Regency Rake' might have been made for him, and probably was. A heavy gambler, who was reputed never to have opened his mouth in the ring for under £500, Mellish lived at Blythe, near Doncaster, and won the Legers of 1804 and 1805 with Sancho and Staveley respectively.

There was now an extra day's racing, the stands were enlarged and the price of admission raised to a guinea as the meeting received the seal of royal approval. This occurred when the Prince of Wales, later George IV, and his brother William, also a future King, attended the race week in 1806. Both cheerfully took lodgings in the town, and the local population were amazed to see the First Gentleman of Europe standing on the balcony of number 15, South Parade, blowing his nose 'just like anybody else'.

The Royal Party saw Fyldener beat fourteen opponents for the St Leger, the biggest field up to then. In 1808, scandal broke when two horses died of poisoning after drinking from the troughs on Town Moor. This later proved to be the work of a Newmarket tout, Daniel Dawson, who was hanged at Cambridge in 1812, in the presence of 12,000 spectators.

In 1813, the St Leger distance was reduced from two miles to one mile, six furlongs and 193 yards. Two more alterations were to follow; the race was run over one mile, six furlongs and 132 yards in 1826, and the present distance of one mile, six furlongs and 127 yards has been fixed since 1970.

When the distance was altered in 1826, the weights were also changed. Colts were set to carry 8st 6lb and fillies 8st 3lb. In 1839, colts' weights were increased by one pound and the fillies' by one pound, only to be changed again in 1862, when the colts were asked to carry 8st 10lb and the fillies 8st 5lb. The present scale is colts 9st, fillies 8st 11lb, as it has been since 1884 when the Lambkin gave Jack Watts the second of his five St Leger winners.

In 1819, the Leger was run twice, as it was to be in 1823. Nineteen runners faced Joseph Lockwood in his capacity as the starter, but when Lockwood dropped his flag, five of them were left, being 'not ready', including Agricola, the joint second favourite. Antonio, ridden by T. Nicholson won the race at 33/1, with the favourite Wrangler second and Archibald third, but an angry crowd protested with such vehemence that the stewards decided to order a re-run, declaring a false start to the first 'race'.

This time, only ten took the field, not in-

FRANK BUCKLE

cluding Antonio. Sir Walter amongst those left the first time, ran out the winner from the luckless Wrangler, with Archibald again third. Agricola was not in the frame, and the whole affair was reported to the Jockey Club. The Stewards of the Club, after examining Lockwood, who was both starter and judge, decided that the original result should stand, with Antonio the winner, declaring that the Doncaster stewards should not have allowed a second race.

In fairness to the local stewards, Mr J.W. Wentworth and Mr Mark Milbank, this decision must have been more easily arrived at in the calm and comfort of the Newmarket Rooms than with a howling mob of Town Moor punters banging on the door.

After the 1821 race had given jockey William Scott, riding Jack Spigot, the first of his nine St Leger winners, events on Town Moor were over-shadowed by a spectacular duel fought to defend a lady's honour at nearby Blythe. Mr 'P-r-r', des-cribed as a gentleman of fortune, challenged Captain 'S---n', after the former considered him-self insulted by the Captain's conduct to a female relative of Mr P's in the grandstand on the Thursday of the meeting.

Pistols for two (and presumably coffee for one) on the Friday morning resulted in the gallant Captain being carried from the field in 'a dan-gerous state' with a pistol ball lodged in his shoulder. Two other protagonists involved in the affair fought a separate duel and managed to miss each other, but reading between the lines, Mr P's unnamed female relative must have been quite a lady.

The St Leger of 1822 saw the winner Theodore start at the incredible odds of 1,000 to 5. The horse had won the Spring St Leger at York, but arrived at Doncaster looking so lame as to be almost a cripple; so much so that his intended rider, John Jackson, burst into tears when told by trainer James Croft that he must ride to win.

Theodore's owner, the Hon. Edward Petre, thought so little of his chances that he sold all his bets to his gambling partner, Rodes Milnes, friend of the Prince Regent and Beau Brummell, and a fearless punter. Both Petre and Milnes were to be broke within a dozen years, but their luck was in on Leger Day 1822. Croft told Jackson to spur Theodore on at flagfall and make every post a winning one, and he was never headed to win by four lengths, giving Jackson his eighth winning Leger ride, and Petre the first of four St Legers. Croft achieved the unique feat of saddling the first four home.

The 7/4 favourite, Swap, was virtually tailed off in the hands of Will Scott, but when Theodore and Swap met again three days later for the Gascoigne Stakes over the same course and dis-tance at level weights with the same jockeys, Swap was the easy winner from his odds-on rival; a result which excited much comment, but no official action.

Whatever the merits or demerits of that par-ticular case, the first half of the nineteenth century was no place for the squeamish where moral values were concerned. Joseph Lockwood faced his severest test as starter in 1827, when several of the jockeys amongst the twenty-six runners de-liberately engineered false starts to foil the hopes of

Marmeluke, the Derby winner owned by prize fighter John Gully. When the field finally got away after the Duke of Devonshire, a steward of the meeting, had been to Lockwood's assistance, Sam Chifney Jnr on Marmeluke was facing the wrong way, and was left a hundred yards. It was impossible to make up the ground, and Mameluke went under by an official length to Edward Petre's Matilda.

Compensation awaited John Gully in 1832, when Jem Robinson, the rider of Matilda in the 1827 race, won for the former pugilist on Margrave. In the same year, Gully had been elected Member of Parliament for Pontefract, an elevation due less to his political skills than his placing of free barrels of beer in the streets for the benefit of a thirsty electorate, but doubtless the £45,000 he took out of the ring over Margrave helped to pay for that.

Events at a dinner party held to celebrate Mr Richard Watt's third St Leger victory with Rockingham, ridden by Sam Darling, in 1833, merely provided light relief; it seems that Mr Watt and his old friend, Sir Tatton Sykes, had seen Rockingham well and truly toasted in port before attempting to join the ladies, and elected to help each other up the staircase to the drawing room; their mutual exertions resulted in a swift and undignified descent of the stairs by both gentlemen no sooner had they reached the top.

The following year, 6/5 on favourite and Derby winner Plenipotentiary was doped so badly that he could barely get to the post, let alone win, although it is doubtful that he could have beaten the winner, Touchstone, even at his best; in

LORD GEORGE BENTINCK

addition to the St Leger, Touchstone won two Doncaster Cups and two Ascot Gold Cups.

The massive clean-up of racing launched by Lord George Bentinck in the 1840s included an exhortation to the Doncaster Corporation to put up at least another £1,000 in support of the races. Lord George's interest in the Yorkshire track doubtless stemmed from the remarkable coup which he landed with Elis in the St Leger of 1836. Although one of the Turf's greatest reformers, Bentinck was not averse to a tilt at the ring, indeed he needed to make his betting pay as his father, the Duke of Portland, though a lover of racing, hated gambling and refused to supply the funds.

Elis was trained at Stockbridge by John Barham Day, and had been beaten in the Guineas by Bay Middleton, at some cost to Bentinck. So Lord George decided to lay the horse out for a gamble in the St Leger. Elis was transferred to the stables of John Kent, trainer to Bentinck's friend, the Duke of Richmond, on the latter's Goodwood estate. This Duke was the son of Colonel Anthony St Leger's associate in Ireland. Bentinck ran Elis as often as he could during the summer, and ten days before the St Leger, Elis was reported to be in his Sussex stable.

Knowing that it was impossible for a horse to walk the 250 miles to Yorkshire in the time, the bookmakers happily laid Bentinck 12/1 for the Leger. Lord George and John Day then transported Elis in a specially constructed van, pulled by six horses at the rate of eighty miles a day and the horse arrived in Doncaster two days before the race. Ridden by John Day, Elis won easily from the 6/4 favourite Scroggins with Bee'swing third. This

JOHN GULLY

must have been a vintage St Leger, as the filly Bee'swing was to win fifty-one races, including four Doncaster Cups, and the Ascot Gold Cup.

Lord George's mood was obviously a little different on Leger day in 1841 when, in addition to demanding the extra £1,000 from the civic coffers, he informed the Corporation that the Jockey Club could see its way to 'annihilate' the Doncaster races, unless the funds were forthcoming. The civic mind, thus wonderfully concentrated, ensured the funds were indeed forthcoming and the undignified process of handing round the Doncaster Cup at the Mansion House dinner to collect guineas for the following season's prize was sensibly abandoned in favour of a more specific contribution.

In 1851, a Ladies' Stand was built to encourage female spectators. This was quite an innovation, as except at Ascot, Goodwood and Newmarket, women received little protection and few went racing.

At about this time, the real success story of the St Leger was rapidly unfolding; the Scott brothers were taking Doncaster by storm. John Scott trained at Whitewall stables in Middleham and no other northern trainer has equalled his record in the classics before or since. His first success in the St Leger with Matilda in 1827 preceded fifteen more Leger wins, and he won five Derbies, nine Oaks, seven Two Thousand Guineas and four One Thousand Guineas – a total of forty-one classic successes, including those of West Australian, first winner of the Triple Crown in 1853.

His brother William was a genius in the saddle, a genius badly tainted and eventually destroyed by his addiction to the bottle. He should have won the Triple Crown on Sir Tatton Sykes, named after the Yorkshire sportsman. Scott trained and rode the horse to win the Two Thousand and the St Leger, but he arrived at the start at Epsom hopelessly drunk on brandy.

Scott was left many lengths while arguing with the starter, but even so Sir Tatton Sykes was beaten only a neck by Pyrrhus the First. Scott had been apprenticed to James Croft, the trainer of Theodore, and with all his faults, Will Scott remains the supreme St Leger jockey; his record of nine wins is unlikely to be equalled, let alone beaten.

Of the eighteen feature races listed on the cards for the second half of the nineteenth century, only seven remain today: the St Leger, the Doncaster Cup, the Scarborough Stakes, the Town Plate (run at the March meeting) the Portland Handicap, the Park Hill Stakes and the Champagne Stakes. In 1871, winning owners of the Champagne Stakes were doubtless pleased to be relieved of the obligation to donate six dozen bottles to the Doncaster Race Club, as had been the case since 1823.

Apart from a visit by the then Princess Victoria in 1835, royal patronage was lacking at Doncaster until 1876, when the Prince of Wales, later Edward VII, became a regular visitor. The Prince won the St Leger with Persimmon in 1896 with Jack Watts up, and again in 1900 when Herbert Jones booted home 7/2 on favourite Diamond Jubilee.

The new century brought with it a new contraption: the starting gate. Introduced for two-year-old races in 1900, it became mandatory except for races over extreme distances in 1901. The gate was to remain in use for well over sixty years, but was rarely popular with jockeys, trainers or horses and it is no surprise to learn that the Leger start was delayed by horses refusing to walk up to the gate.

The 1901 race was a scrappy affair, won by Kempton Cannon on Leopold de Rothschild's Doricles from Lester Reiff on the Derby winner,

Volodyovski. Both jockeys were riding in the American 'crouch' style that had recently been made popular by Tod Sloan. Reiff objected to the winner for bumping, but this was overruled, and Doricles kept the race at 40/1 with Volodyovski returned 6/5 on favourite.

The following year was that of the extraordinary filly Sceptre. A daughter of Persimmon, she was one of the most successful horses ever to look through a bridle, winning four classics and finishing fourth in the Derby.

Ridden by Fred Hardy, she won the St Leger easily by three lengths, at 100/30. Pulled out again two days later for the Park Hill Stakes, she started at 4/1 on but was trounced by Elba, a filly she had left for dead in the Oaks.

But Sceptre had been subjected to a hard season by her gambling owner-trainer, Robert Sievier. She began her classic preparation by running second in the Lincolnshire Handicap, which would be unthinkable today especially for a filly who had won the July Stakes at Newmarket and the Woodcote Stakes at Epsom as a two-year-old. The Lincolnshire, then run at the now defunct Lincoln course, and run at Doncaster since 1965, was followed by victories in the One Thousand and Two Thousand Guineas, a hard race in the Derby and a win in the Oaks. Then came another hard race in Paris to finish second in the Grand Prix, two races in two days at Ascot, winning the St James's Palace Stakes, and two races at Goodwood, winning the Nassau Stakes.

Horses had to be tough in those days, and Sceptre was brave as well, but she had looked all skin and bone when she won the St Leger, and her

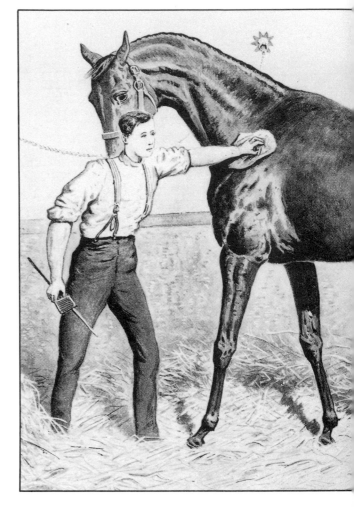

Park Hill defeat surprised no one except Sievier.

Writing in 1903, F.H. Bayles said, 'Races on the old Town Moor of Doncaster even to the present day, as in time of yore, are an especial feature in the annals of British sport, unexcelled, if equalled, by the Royal favours which are annually bestowed upon the meeting and the general representative assembly from the blue book of united Yorkshire. It would be quite safe to say that on the great St Leger day every family in the peerage of England, Ireland and Scotland has some lineal representative on Town Moor. You may compare it with Ascot socially, you may regard the multitude which congregate on the Epsom Downs, but I feel certain, that were an

PERSIMMON IN WINTER QUARTERS, 1897

actual census taken of the three places, Doncaster would be found to hold its own with Royal Ascot, and take precedence from both a sporting and social aspect, of any race meeting in the United Kingdom. It really is amazing how admirably the enormous concourse of humanity is controlled, and the excessive vehicular traffic regulated'.

Going on to describe the conformation of the track, Bayles describes the first two furlongs of the St Leger course as 'somewhat lumpy' and recommends that, 'considering the enormous revenue that must be forthcoming from these races, the Sandal Mile and other courses thereon should be made perfectly straight'. He further comments: 'His Majesty's horse Lucknow (Tod Sloan)

would never have beaten Eager (Morny Cannon) in the Portland Plate of 1900 but for the favourable curves in the course to the inside position'.

The race was run on the Red House Inn course over an extended five furlongs. Since Sloan was a brilliantly innovative American rider with a crouch style that made Mornington Cannon look like a policeman, the bend in the track about two furlongs from home may not have made that much difference. Nevertheless, Bayles's point was well made and the Sandal course was straightened a few years before the First World War.

1904 saw Pretty Polly complete the One Thousand Guineas, Oaks and St Leger treble. This is often referred to erroneously as 'The Fillies' Triple Crown' (which it cannot be, as all five classics are open to fillies; the colts are confined to the Two Thousand, the Derby and the St Leger, and those three races constitute the Triple Crown for both sexes). Pretty Polly joined a select band of nine racemares to achieve this feat, the latest being Oh So Sharp in 1985.

The shadows of war were lengthening as the moody Black Jester won the 1914 St Leger by five lengths to give jockey Walter Griggs his second Leger victory; the course was closed in 1915, and the St Leger moved to Newmarket, where it was run for the duration of the war as the September Stakes. The race would have been known as the New St Leger but for the extraordinary attitude of the Doncaster Race Committee who announced in June 1915 that 'whenever the St Leger is run it will be at Doncaster'.

Racing resumed on Town Moor in 1919 and Brownie Carslake piloted Kaysoe to victory in the famous black and white colours of Lord Derby. Carslake was a brilliant jockey, born in Australia, and he rode his first winner in England at Birmingham on a horse called The Swagman during a brief visit in 1906. A career in Europe made him champion jockey of Austria-Hungary and on the outbreak of war he fled to Russia, where he became champion jockey in 1916. The 1917 Revolution drove him to England, with his life savings in Russian roubles, only to find the currency worthless.

These vicissitudes were perhaps far from his thoughts as Carslake had the leg-up on Salmon Trout for the 1924 St Leger. The horse was winner of the Princess of Wales' Stakes and the Dewhurst, but being bred by that precocious horse, The Tetrarch, Carslake was convinced he would not stay the Leger distance.

This was a curious assumption, as Salmon Trout was stoutly bred on the dam's side, and The Tetrarch had already sired two Leger winners. Even so, Carslake instructed a bookmaker and close friend, Moe Tarsh, to lay Salmon Trout to lose a very considerable sum on his behalf.

Like many a betting jockey before and since, Carslake now found himself in an invidious position. He was riding for the Aga Khan, one of the richest men in the world, and Carslake enjoyed a huge retainer from the Aga. Although like most rich men His Highness was mean over small matters and reputedly took time to consider whether to give his golf caddy two shillings or a half-crown tip in the year that Bahram won the Triple Crown, he was very generous to any jockey who won a great race for him.

On the other hand, Moe Tarsh had spread the word as he laid Salmon Trout to lose a fortune, and no bookmaker expected the horse to win. In the end Carslake's mind was made up for him. The Doncaster stewards got wind of the affair, and informed the jockey that his riding in the St Leger would be closely watched.

As the race developed, it seemed at first that Carslake could not win; last out of the gate, Salmon Trout still trailed the field with seven furlongs to run. At this point, Carslake started to improve his position, and despite some bunching on the turn, Salmon Trout got a good run up the inside. The

THE ST LEGER FINISH – PRETTY POLLY WINS WITH EASE, 1904

favourite Polyphontes weakened two furlongs from home and Santorb, ridden by George Hulme, looked the likely winner until Salmon Trout came with a superb late run to get up in the last hundred yards and win by two lengths.

Like many Australians, Carslake was a superb judge of pace and fourteen years later won the best St Leger run in the 1930s, the 1938 renewal. Pasch was favourite to win for Gordon Richards as he had in the Two Thousand Guineas, although being no better than third in the Derby. Carslake and Scottish Union had finished second in both races, but Pasch was 6/5 with Scottish Union at 7/2.

In contrast to Salmon Trout's race, Carslake waited in from half-way up the straight, never having been worse than second. Eph Smith on Challenge tackled Scottish Union with everything they had in the final furlong, but Carslake coolly coaxed Scottish Union home by a neck, never resorting to the whip.

The outbreak of World War II on 3rd September, 1939 denied Eph Smith certain consolation on his Derby winner, Blue Peter. Town Moor became a depot for the Royal Army Veterinary Corps for the duration of the war, and ambitious plans for rebuilding John Carr's 1777 grandstands had to be

THE AGA KHAN'S ST LEGER WITH FIRDAUSSI,
1932

shelved. The St Leger had various homes: Thirsk, Manchester, Newmarket and York.

In the immediate post-war years, Doncaster enjoyed the boom generated by thousands of recently demobilised servicemen with gratuities to spend before the austerity of the new Labour Government began to bite. Over a hundred thousand spectators crowded the enclosures to see Airborne supplement his Derby victory in the hands of Tommy Lowrey, thus becoming the only grey to win both the Derby and the Leger. It was two hours before the traffic cleared the course after racing, but thousands stayed on Town Moor to enjoy a carnival of pre-war standards and the only missing element was the traditional Doncaster Butterscotch; this was still the era of sweet rationing.

The next two St Legers were won by Edgar Britt, an Australian jockey with an exaggerated crouch style which made Tod Sloan seem like Fred Archer. It was, however, very effective and Britt won the 1947 race on Sayajirao for the last of the Indian potentates, the Gaekwar of Baroda, and in 1948 rode Black Tarquin to victory in the colours of the Chairman of the New York Jockey Club, William Woodward.

The French invasion, which was such a feature of top class racing in post-war England, was at its height when Marcel Boussac's Scratch II, with Rae Johnstone up, won from his compatriot Vieux Manoir in 1950; but this was the last Leger to fall to the French for twenty-six years. Meld completed the One Thousand, Oaks and St Leger treble in 1955, and in 1970 Nijinsky became the last horse to win the Triple Crown in the hands of Lester Piggott, who was to ride eight Leger winners.

In the 1970s, it was considered by some observers that the St Leger had lost its appeal, and was in danger of becoming a mediocre event, a view that was strengthened when the handicapper Peleid won in 1973. The suggestion that the race

PERSONALITIES ON THE TOWN MOOR

should be opened to older horses was firmly resisted, a decision amply rewarded when Her Majesty's Dunfermline completed the Oaks and St Leger double in 1977.

Doncaster has changed somewhat from the Edwardian heyday described so eloquently by F.H. Bayles. There is little Royal patronage, although the Queen did attend the bicentenary celebrations and has made the occasional private visit from her holiday home in Balmoral. You could probably fire off a cannon in the grandstand without hitting a lineal descendant of the peerage, but that isn't to say that Doncaster on Leger Day has lost any of its colour and excitement.

Corporate entertainment may have replaced the coronets, but old Sir Tatton Sykes, who gave his name to the 1846 winner, witnessed seventy-six Legers in his ninety-one years and must rate as Doncaster's number one fan of all time. He would still be proud to be on hand for the North's greatest race.

Sir Tatton would have a little difficulty in recognising the modern stands which replaced John Carr's buildings in 1969 after nearly two hundred years of service, but he would certainly relish the carnival atmosphere and the warmth of the welcome extended in what the sporting baronet would have known as the West Riding of Yorkshire.

They may run them in Kentucky, they may run them in France, in Ireland, Italy and Argentina; they probably run them in Serbo-Croatia, but Doncaster is where it all started, on Cantley Common hard by Town Moor, the home of the world's oldest classic race. ■

LESTER PIGGOTT WINS ON STORM WARNING, 1985

NEWCASTLE

Now lads and lasses myed for toon,
And in the road they oft lay doon,
Faith! monny a lassie spoil'd her goon,
A Comin frae the Races O.

Some gat hyem, midst outs and ins,
Some had black eyes and broken shins,
And some lay drunk among the whins,
A Comin frae the Races O.   (Geordie song)

SUCH WAS the low life of Newcastle races, probably founded in the early seventeenth century on Killingworth Moor, transferring to the Town Moor in 1721. The odd meeting was still occasionally held at Killingworth, but the parsimonious corporation had refused to pay for 'cords', i.e. rails, hence the move.

The conditions on Town Moor were a little on the primitive side, with a contemporary observer noting that the 'erection of coarse boards', which passed for a stand, 'neither protects the company from the wind nor weather and where every squall endangers the necks of the occupiers'.

All this was to change under the administration of William Loftus, appointed Clerk of the Course in 1789 by the Corporation officials hitherto responsible for running the meeting. Loftus used the then normal device of issuing fifteen-guinea silver badges, giving perpetual admission to Town Moor as a way of raising the capital for a proper grandstand, erected in 1800 and described at the time as 'being as convenient and commodious as could be wished'. Unfortunately the meeting was spoiled on this particular occasion by the behaviour of two 'gentlemen' indulging in high words over some old fox hunting

quarrel; thus proving themselves no better than the low lifers 'drunk among the whins' described above.

The stand was of such substance that when racing was moved to the present site at Higher Gosforth Park in 1882, it became Bishop Chadwick's Roman Catholic Memorial School, but meanwhile Town Moor had witnessed the founding of the race which became known in the South as 'The Pitmen's Derby' but always known in Northumberland simply and rightly as 'The Plate'.

First run in 1833, as a £15 handicap sweepstakes with £100 added and won by Tomboy, the Northumberland Plate over two miles quickly caught the imagination of the punters and the racing fraternity alike; which was just as well. Since 1811 Newcastle had slumped badly in popular esteem, being considered a venue for 'third raters' in *The Sporting Magazine*'s review of the 1832 season.

By 1838, the four-day meeting held at the end of June, known locally as 'The Noodles', was re-established. James Whyte was able to recommend visits to the Newcastle Literary and Philosophical Society, the Antiquarian Society, and the Theatre Royal as a selection of diversions for racegoers relaxing after a day watching the magical mare, Bee'swing, clean up one of her six Gold Cups, plus the Craven Stakes and the Plate.

The revival was principally due to the efforts of James Radford, the Clerk of the Course. The Gold Cup was won in the 1840s by such superb animals as the great mare Alice Hawthorn, ridden by Sim Templeman and said to have 'an action like a hare, stealing along the ground with her ears pricked'. But the 'Filthy Forties' took their toll of corruption in the North-East as elsewhere. In 1852, *The Sportsman* was complaining of the number of ante-post fancies suddenly withdrawn before the start, presumably with the connivance of owners and bookmakers. By 1862 the problem had become chronic, described by *Baily's Magazine* as 'an unblushing and disreputable robbery perpetrated by the owners of the animals engaged in the Northumberland Plate'.

Corruption having stained Newcastle racing as black as your hat, and with crime also becoming endemic in the racegoers, the only solution was to move the fixture from the horrors of Town Moor to the haven of Higher Gosforth, a beautiful park owned by the Brandling family.

Attendance was poor at the inaugural meeting in 1882, run in blazing heat with hay-making taking prior claim on the potential punters, but eventually all was well. Fred Archer made a rare appearance to win the 1883 Northumberland Plate on Barcaldine, carrying 9st 7lb while conceding seventeen pounds to Shrewsbury, ridden by the local hero Johnny Osborne. So the meeting thrived in the pleasing ambience of what has become a thousand-acre leisure park.

A wider range of competitive long-distance handicaps has reduced the Northumberland Plate's role in the modern racing scene, but the Geordie crowds still head for Gosforth to celebrate the running of 'The Plate' in the identical sporting spirit which induced their forebears in 1738 to stage a race for asses 'to be rode by chimney sweeps, and their brushes to pay them along'. ■

PONTEFRACT

'O Pomfret, Pomfret! O thou bloody prison,
Fatal and ominous to noble peers!
Within the guilty closure of thy walls
Richard the Second here was hack'd to death;
And for more slander to thy dismal seat,
We give to thee our guiltless blood to drink.'

SO SAID Earl Rivers, according to Shakespeare's *Richard III*, as he prepared to meet his end within the bloodstained walls of Pomfret Castle in 1485.

As the wretched Rivers indicated, he was not the first, nor was he the last, to die at the castle. It was originally built on the orders of William the Conqueror by Ilbert de Lacy in the town now better known as Pontefract, which itself was originally called Kirkby but was renamed by the Normans after a broken bridge crossing the Humber.

During the Civil War, Pontefract Castle was considered to be 'the key to the North', and this Royalist stronghold was laid siege to by the Roundheads twice before Colonel John Morris was forced to seek an honourable surrender on behalf of the King's forces, only to be retaken by the gallant Colonel in an operation of which the S.A.S. would have been proud.

All this bloodshed was too much for the good citizens of Pontefract, who preferred to concentrate on the manufacture of the famous liquorice cake, invented in 1562. Lacking the courage and spirit of Colonel Morris, the burgesses of the town deserted the King's cause and petitioned for the castle 'to be wholly razed down and demolished'. Cromwell's men were only too happy to

oblige, and in 1649 the historic six-hundred-year-old castle lay in ruins.

Astonishingly, racing had taken place between sieges, in March 1648, but it was to be ninety years before the *Racing Calendar* of 1738 was able to record another meeting, a rather mean affair, with a £30 plate for six-year-olds the principal race. Pontefract remained swathed in self-imposed obscurity until the turn of the century, when Lord Darlington was the chief patron of a three-day meeting held in 1801.

The timing of the races was shrewdly judged. Taking place in August, between the York summer meeting and the Doncaster St Leger week, many horses ran at Pontefract en route from the Knavesmire to Town Moor.

A Gold Cup was run for the first time in 1802, and won by Lord Darlington's Muley Moloch, beaten by Quiz in the previous season's St Leger. In the same year a grandstand was built by the subscription of £50 for silver badges giving free entry to the stand for twenty years. Darlington's patronage barely survived this period, although he won four Gold Cups and rode the course himself as an amateur, but his place was taken by no less a sporting figure than the Hon. Edward Petre, in 1816, who inherited nearby Stapleton Hall and a fortune to match. Petre organised race meetings at Stapleton for amateur riders to amuse his many sporting friends, including the Prince Regent.

In the same year, his four-year-old filly Agatha won the Pontefract Gold Cup, and in 1822 he inaugurated a spring meeting on the Pontefract course for the benefit of members of the Badsworth Hunt, of which he became Master.

Pontefract

Also in 1816, The Duchess won the Gold Cup before going on to victory in the St Leger in the elegant hands of Ben Smith, and in 1823 Dr Syntax, later to become a famous stallion and winner of thirty-six races in all, set a record by winning his twentieth Gold Cup.

That season, Squire Richard Watt of Bishop Burton, near Beverley, gave his colt Barefoot an airing at Pontefract before a St Leger victory under Tom Goodisson.

Although never likely to supersede its more distinguished neighbours at York and Doncaster, Pontefract seemed set to enjoy long popularity, with good fields and good horses; but it was not to be. By 1834, Edward Petre was broke, his fortune swallowed up by gambling. Worn out with debt, he sold Stapleton and quit the Turf. Without his patronage, Pontefract went into decline and racing ceased in 1835, although the Badsworth Hunt continued the March meeting as a steeplechasing fixture.

Pontefract flickered into life again in 1852, but the real fire had gone and the sport was only moderate. The Corporation acquired the land in 1906, but were reluctant to improve either the quality of the racing or the amenities, and it was only when the Jockey Club threatened to withdraw the licence that the matter was reconsidered, to become merely academic when the First World War intervened.

The Kaiser defeated, new stands were built in 1919 and racing resumed under the formidable command of Brigadier-General Sir Loftus Bates on behalf of a newly formed Pontefract Racecourse Company. The course soon gained in popularity, with increased prize money and improved facilities, and although the track was threatened with subsidence from coal mining activities in the early sixties, it has continued to prosper.

The course was plagued with hard summer going for many years, but by liaison with a local colliery in 1980, a watering system was installed and in 1983 the horseshoe left-handed track was restored to its original two-mile circuit.

Pontefract now attracts plenty of runners from the South, notably from Newmarket, and the mineworkers' shift times ensure that racing rarely starts before 2.45, thus allowing a leisurely luncheon. Set in the industrial heartland of Yorkshire, Pontefract will never again be 'the beautiful picturesque racing ground' described in *The Sporting Magazine* in 1802; but it is one of the friendliest racecourses in the author's experience, and it must not be forgotten that Pontefract was one of the few tracks to continue racing during the Second World War, when it became the temporary home of both the Lincolnshire and the Manchester November Handicaps, meetings being held every other Saturday throughout the season. Thus 'Ponte' did its bit to relieve the tedium of powdered egg, Woolton pie and whisky 'for regulars only', even if you could get the Pomfret cakes on your sweet ration. ∎

REDCAR

WHEN Her Royal Highness the Princess Anne rode Gulfland into the winners' enclosure at Redcar in August 1986 following a five-length victory in the Mommessin Stakes, the lady now known as the Princess Royal was putting the Cleveland course into the record books for the second time in two years.

For Gulfland was the first winner under Rules to be ridden by a member of the Royal Family since Charles II scored at the Newmarket Spring Meeting in 1675. There can be little doubt that the Merry Monarch would have celebrated in style that evening and scored again in the welcoming arms of Mistress Gwyn!

There can be no doubt, however, that Provideo established the twentieth-century record for two-year-old wins in a season when chalking up his sixteenth victory on 1st November, 1984. In fact it is to be considered as an all-time record, since The Bard's sixteen wins in 1855 included a walk-over.

It is an interesting reflection on the disparity of racing then and now. The Bard went on to be second in the Derby to Ormonde, win the Goodwood and Doncaster Cups, and enjoyed a distinguished stud career in France; Provideo ran only three times as a three-year-old, never won again and retired to stud in Tasmania.

Racing at Redcar originally took place on the sands in the bracing air of the north-east coast. The judge officiated from the insecurity of a bathing machine buffeted by a wind which can make a sunny August day feel like Doncaster in March and the elements must have had a considerable effect on the results.

Little money was to hand, as no admission could be charged, and the sports were sensibly moved inland in 1872, when a Redcar Race Company was formed and a course laid down on land leased from Mr A.H.T. Newcomen.

For six shillings, a 'grandstand' patron could command a view from the wooden stand, while if he preferred the comfort of his carriage, the fee was five shillings for a four-wheeler, or half-a-crown for a two-wheeled conveyance. For tuppence, the humbler racegoer might enjoy the freedom of the infield.

In 1876, a proper grandstand was erected, under the auspices of the Redcar and Coatham Grandstand Company, chaired by Mr Newcomen. A brief flirtation with National Hunt racing was ended in 1878 after a day spoiled by small fields and fighting jockeys. They were gentlemen riders, at that, who should have known better in the decorous atmosphere of the town which devised that epitome of Victorian modesty, the bathing machine.

Indeed, as James Gill points out in his *Racecourses*, published in 1975, the correspondent of *Baily's Magazine* found Redcar 'the one spot left in the seaside life of England whither German bands came not, nor nigger ministrelsy; where there are no bazaars, or wheels of fortune; no open work stockings, and no Lesbias to too tightly lace their robes of gold.'

Which presumably left only a day at the races to amuse the lighter hearted citizen, who was richly rewarded for his patronage as well-endowed races brought the top racing names of the day to fight it out around Redcar's narrow oval circuit.

Redcar

GEORGE FORDHAM

Fred Archer, George Fordham and Jack Watts were all happy to make the trek up from Newmarket before Redcar's fortunes slumped in the industrial decline of the late nineteenth century.

Newcomen died in 1884, and the Marquis of Zetland, long a patron, became Chairman. A very experienced Clerk of the Course, Miles I'Anson was appointed and Redcar survived to provide unambitious racing fare for the next sixty years, discounting wartime interruptions.

In 1946, Major Leslie Petch, M.F.H., became Managing Director and Clerk of the Course. In theatrical circles, Petch would have been known as a 'play-doctor', the man the management send for when all seems lost and the production doomed. 'Course-doctor' doesn't sound quite right; perhaps 'witch-doctor' might be more appropriate, because Petch worked magic as an administrator, not only at York and Catterick, but also at Redcar, perhaps his finest achievement.

Expert in attracting sponsors, especially in the early days of I.T.V. coverage, Petch transformed Redcar with a meticulous attention to detail, mostly on behalf of the patrons of the cheaper rings, and provided decent catering, colourful racecards and proper seating. The Vaux Gold Tankard, first run in 1959, was for a time Europe's richest handicap, and the level of prize money, which stood at £8,450 in 1946, had become £72,550 by 1964.

Major Petch's efforts were rewarded when the Levy Board advanced over a quarter of a million pounds for a new grandstand, opened in 1964. Twenty-five years on, Redcar is receiving another facelift, with two million pounds spent on a new stable block, lads' hostel and stand improvements. As at Ayr, Newbury and Newcastle, the work is being financed by the sale of surplus land.

It's all a far cry from blustery beaches and blown-down bathing vans, which must have afforded the spectators what Lord Lonsdale used to call 'lots of lovely fun'; the words of Lord Tennyson are also appropriate: 'The sands and yeasty surges mix in caves about the dreary bay'. Modern Redcar, however, is 'lovely fun', too. ■

# RIPON

UNEASY LIES the head that wears the crown, as King Henry IV wisely remarked, and in 1405 Bolingbroke's bonce was even more restless as the plague swept through London. The King elected to take refuge in the ancient city of Ripon, which was not a good decision for a troubled sleeper, as the Wakeman observed the now thousand-year-old custom of blasting his horn in the market place and outside the Mayor's house to reassure the citizens that the local vigilantes considered all to be well and peaceful.

Later monarchs also passed through, including James I and Charles I, the latter receiving a pair of Ripon Rowells as a gesture of admiration from the city's time-honoured spur-making craftsmen. The spurs were so finely made that they gave rise to the phrase 'as true as Ripon Rowells', meaning a man of integrity; and there could not have been a better recipient than that tragic king.

The first recorded race meeting was twenty years later, on Bondgate Green in 1664, and subsequently took place at five other locations before being established on the present site in 1900.

Mouncton, or Monkton, Moor, High Common, Red Banks and the field behind Mr Haygarth's pub all sufficed to keep the local sportsmen, and women, interested. In 1723 Ripon staged the first race confined to lady riders when Mrs Aislabie, wife of John Aislabie, an influential citizen, gave a Plate 'to be run for by women'.

This amiable piece of mild titillation horrified one local commentator, who wrote:

'Mrs Aislabie gave a Plate to be run for by women and nine of the sex rid astride, dressed in drawers and waistcoats, and jockey caps, their shapes transparent. I think the lady benefactress to this indecent diversion, should have made the tenth.'

Well perhaps Mrs Aislabie thought it wasn't quite the thing to race for her own prize, or perhaps she modestly considered her 'shape transparent' not worthy of display. What is certain is that the event packed High Common and the author wishes he'd been around to do the commentary.

Not even John Fairfax-Blakeborough could remember that period, but this finest of northern Turf historians was at his best when, towards the end of his long life, he looked back on racing at tracks such as Ripon in the late nineteenth and early twentieth centuries.

'They were very pleasant, the leisurely days of yore, when race meetings could be run at little cost; when they were much more in the nature of an open air club at which hunting men and horse lovers met to enjoy each other's society, without expecting much in the way of comfort or amenities. Those days have gone, and with them possibly some of the atmosphere which was so delightful because it was more sporting than commercial.'

Perhaps a little of that sporting spirit still survives at Ripon, one of the best kept and most attractive courses in England, where they remember the Wakeman with a two-and-a-quarter mile handicap, the Ripon Rowells with a one mile handicap, and the city's patron saint is commemorated with the Great St Wilfrid Handicap, one of the season's most competitive six-furlong races. ∎

THE 'WIRELESS' OF RACING: THE ART OF
TICTACKING, 1923

THIRSK

'One of those pretty little meetings, such as we fall in with only in Yorkshire, which commence after dinner, close in time for middle-class tea, and amuse all classes of the community.'

THUS VAN DRIVER of *Baily's Magazine* found Thirsk in the early 1860s, a few years after the evening in 1854 when a local landowner, Squire Frederick Bell of Thirsk Hall, enjoyed a convivial session in the Golden Fleece Hotel with a few chums and decided to stage a meeting on his hard-by estate.

The prime object was to have a bit of fun, and inexpensive fun at that, with runners stabled at local inns. This was not as cheapjack as it sounds, since Thirsk is well endowed with hostelries, and on a clear night you can spot nine from the porch of the Golden Fleece. But the two-day meetings held subsequent to the inaugural gathering on 15th March, 1855 had to rub by on a total income of £700, including prize money.

The Clerk of the Scales weighed the jockeys with a gadget intended to gauge the poundage of potato sacks, and the Clerk of the Course was the schoolmaster, George Nicholson, who survived twenty years in the post until he came up on the Autumn Double with Duke of Parma in the Cesarewitch at 4/1 and Sutton in the Cambridgeshire, carrying 5st 13lbs at 3/1. Both were favourites, and, unprepared by a lifetime of teaching Caesar's Gallic Wars to the unresponsive youth of Thirsk, he died of sheer exhilaration.

This unhappy event signalled the end of Thirsk's cheerful amateurism, and Thomas Dawson Jnr was appointed Clerk of the Course. His father Tom Dawson Snr was a Middleham trainer who won five classics, including the Derby with Ellington in 1856. On his way back from Epsom, the absent-minded Dawson left the £25,000 he had taken off the bookies in an aged hat-box when he changed trains at Northallerton, but he advertised for its return stating that the box contained 'nothing of interest to anyone except the owner' and was lucky enough to have his property restored intact.

Dawson Jnr had also enjoyed a distinguished training career, producing Tom Whiffler to win the Chester Cup in 1862 from his stables in the Hambleton Hills, eight miles from Thirsk. Racing had been recorded here since 1612 when James I donated a gold cup for the Royal Plate. In so doing, he founded the Hambleton Cup, a two-mile race still run today, although reduced in distance to a mile and a half.

In the event, Dawson was to prove a better administrator than a trainer and swiftly built a reputation for enterprise which was to stand him in good stead at Redcar, Lanark, Haydock and York where he also officiated. He took the bull by the horns at Thirsk and boosted prize money in a manner which had the die-hards taking a sharp intake of breath, but attracted the trainers from the nearby centres of Malton, Middleham, Hambleton, Richmond and Beverley.

The growth of the railways brought southern-trained competitors as well and all continued happily until 1914; after the war, the buildings were dilapidated and the course unraceable. In 1924, the North's leading racing impressario, Brigadier-General Sir Loftus Bates, restored the

Thirsk

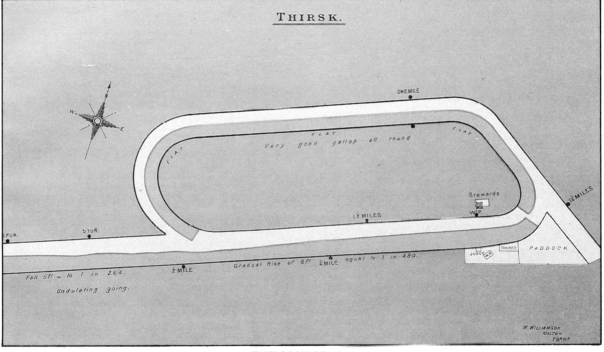

THE COURSE, 1903

course under the auspices of a newly formed Race Company of which he was Managing Director, and as with all the Bates enterprises, success was swiftly assured after the track re-opened on the 8th August, 1924.

In 1940, Thirsk saw the running of the substitute St Leger, called the Yorkshire St Leger. It was won by Gordon Richards on Turkhan at 4/1 from his more fancied stable companion Stardust, the 9/4 favourite piloted by Harry Wragg in the first colours of the winning owner, H.H. Aga Khan; proving once again that there is nothing new in Eastern potentates attempting to monopolise top-class races.

Post war, Bates's successor, Lt. Col. J.W. Johnson, who had had considerable experience of racecourse administration while serving in the Indian Army, founded the Classic Trial Stakes as a one thousand pounds event. Although today's prize of £5,526 is less valuable in real terms, the race has survived many better endowed early 'classic' trials and attracts good-quality fields to this friendly course, as does the Thirsk Hunt Cup and the historic Hambleton Cup, all run on Saturdays at a track particularly well off for week-end fixtures. ∎

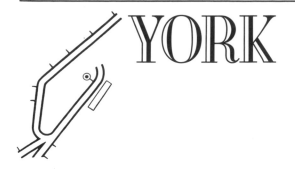

YORK

'York lads are fond of running horses.'
Richard Brinsley Sheridan, *The School for Scandal*

LUCIUS SEPTIMUS SEVERUS, Emperor of Rome, liked nothing better in his off-duty moments than a bit of action at the Coliseum or the Circus Maximus, where the horses raced in teams distinguished by coloured streamers flying from the saddles and harness. Severus watched from the luxury of huge baths built into his private stand as the horses were led into the starting gates on the all-weather track.

As starting stalls were not introduced in Britain until 1965 and all-weather tracks have only just come into operation, Severus might have been forgiven a twinge of irritation with the backward British as he wearily donned his purple and gold armoured uniform and set out with his army in the year 208 to restore order in colonial Britain.

Severus was distracted from the local form book by the news that the Caledonians had breached Hadrian's Wall and annihilated the Ninth Legion. He was sixty-two years old and wracked with terminal illness as he led his troops into the fortress of Eboracum.

To provide recreation for the garrison, the patricians, and the usual horde of civil servants, Severus brought several teams of Arab horses, and on an area known much later as the Knavesmire, team horse racing in the Roman style was staged. The meetings were well supported, betting was heavy and as you would expect from the Romans, impeccably ruled and professionally organised.

Severus was buried at Eboracum, the first

LUCIUS SEPTIMUS SEVERUS

Roman Emperor to die in Britain.

He failed to defeat the tiresome Scots, leaving his son and successor as Emperor, Caracalla, to yield up some territory and negotiate a peace that was to last until the Saxons came onto the scene seventy years later. But he bequeathed to York a tradition of horse racing that has survived for eighteen hundred years.

Robert Black, in his *History of Horse Racing in England*, says, 'It is reasonably believed there has always been some kind of horse racing from the very earliest moment at which there were two horses and two Yorkshiremen in the County of Ridings'. But the next recorded event is in 1530, when a silver bell was awarded to Oswald Wyllesthorpe, Esquyer [*sic*] having defeated the nag of William Mallory in a race at what seems to have been a regular fixture in the Forest of Galtres, outside the city walls.

Going was always a problem in the low-lying Vale of York, and the races held on the Rive Ouse,

York

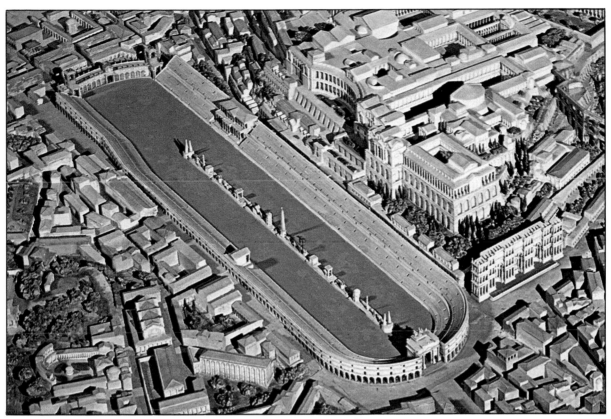

CIRCUS MAXIMUS

frozen in the cruel winter of 1607, may have come as a welcome relief to plodding through the mire. By the time King Charles I dropped in to stay with his friend Sir Henry Slingsby at the Red House, Marston Moor in 1633, the racing was staged on Acomb Moor. His Majesty attended the races on the moor two miles outside the city and was the last reigning monarch to go racing at York until Her Majesty the Queen paid a visit in 1972.

Sir Henry had a winner that day, and as the King and his host celebrated the victory they could not have even considered that eleven years later the battle of Marston Moor would turn the tide of the Civil War in favour of Cromwell and they would both lose their heads in the Royalist cause. Still less would they have believed that they would both be victims of Slingsby's Yorkshire neighbour Sir John Bourchier. Bourchier was a signatory to the King's death warrant, and arrested Slingsby and handed him over to the Puritans.

Oliver Cromwell was no friend of racing, or any other pastime which remotely suggested enjoyment, and although there may have been racing at York after the Restoration in 1660, no records exist prior to 1709, when the principal sports were held over Clifton and Rawcliffe Ings on the banks of the River Ouse with minor meetings at the Knavesmire. On Tuesday, 13th September, four horses ran three four-mile heats at the Ings to decide the outcome of a Gold Cup, value fifty guineas. Mr Metcalfe's Wart won the first two heats and the Cup, but was too exhausted to finish better than a 'distanced' (i.e. tailed off) last in the final heat. Under the rules at this time, the owner of the horse which had finished second to Wart in the first two heats and won the third, Mr Heblethwaite's Stout, claimed the stakes.

It was to be eighteen years before John Cheyne's *Racing Calendar* kept an annual record of horse racing, but the York city archives reveal that a Richard Tennant sent the following eye-witness report:

First Day: Was a Golden Cup, 50 Guineas, run for by:

1. Col. Norclif. Distanced ye first heat.
2. Mr Metcalf, of Sandhutton. Wonne ye Cup.
3. Mr Hepplethwaite, Nigh Malton. Ye Stakes
4. Mr Wilks, Nigh Richmond.

They rid eleven stone. Horses six years old.

John Orton, a man who figures large in York racing history fleshed out these bare bones in his *Turf Annals*, published in 1844.

Two days later, four horses met for the £10 Plate, once again in four-mile heats. On this occasion, Button won the first heat with Milkmaid third, and Milkmaid won the second heat with Button taking the minor honours, Brisk finishing second in both heats. In the final and deciding heat, 'Button and Milkmaid came in so near together that it could not be decided by the Tryers; and the riders showing foul play in running, and afterwards fighting on horseback, the plate was given to Mr Graham'.

Mr Graham was the owner of Brisk. There was no Jockey Club at this time and the rules were peculiar to individual meetings. The Tryers were the judges whose duties were not simply to determine the outcome of a race, but to rule in the event of foul play, and their decision in favour of Brisk, who had finished third in the final heat, seems justified.

The meeting prospered and that great racing enthusiast Queen Anne donated a 100 guinea Gold Cup in 1711. The following year Her Majesty sent her grey gelding Pepper to try to win the cash back for the Royal coffers but Pepper could do no better than third after two heats, victory going to a dun horse called Farmer, with another grey, Sturdy Lump, in second. They knew how to name horses in those days, before the black gold spilled out of the deserts of the Middle East centuries later, and the names of many thoroughbreds became unpronounceable to European tongues.

Queen Anne gained some compensation when her bay horse, Star, won a £14 Plate on Friday, 30th July, 1714, but by this time the founder of Royal Ascot was close to death. On Monday, 2nd August, the news of her demise reached York, and following the proclamation of the new King, George I, by Archbishop Dawes, the nobility and the gentry left for London. However, racing continued and the six-day meeting was concluded after Bagpiper had won a £40 Plate on the following day.

The state of the going remained a problem. Even in August the Ouse frequently burst its banks, as it does today, and by 1730 the situation at Clifton Ings had become impossible. The City of York's administrators had sensibly anticipated the difficulty and engaged Alderman John Telford, an expert gardener and seedsman, to design and lay down a proper course on Emperor Severus's old stamping ground on the Knavesmire, where racing had been resumed in 1709 on a muddy terrain which the Emperor would have found familiar.

The land had derived its name from the public executions held there since 1379, and the City

76

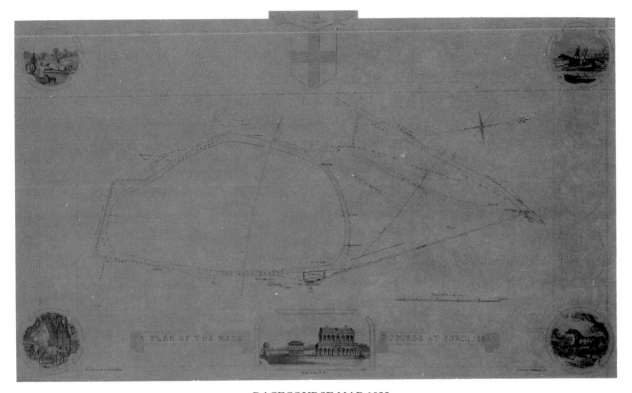

RACECOURSE MAP, 1855

burghers were no fools, realising that the tabloid mentality of the average citizen who attended the morning executions would guarantee a good crowd for the racing in the afternoon. This would be ably supplemented by the nobility and gentry bored with life at the interminably dull Hanoverian court of George II; to say nothing of the ladies who found a vicarious thrill in the best traditions of 'The Wicked Lady' as 'lovable' rogues like Dick Turpin swung for their sins.

Telford's job was not easy, but his work has stood the test of time, excepting for a loop in the course known as the Basin, between the twelve-furlong and two-mile starts, intended to provide for four-mile races, it being impossible at the time to make an oval track. For all Telford's efforts, drainage work was to continue for many years and the state of the terrain made the loop dangerous. It finally fell into disuse, although clearly shown in the map of 1855.

This was in the future, as Lord Lonsdale's Monkey cantered to the post for the King's Plate of 100 guineas, run in two heats for six-year-olds carrying 12st. It was the first day of a six-day meeting commencing on 16th August, 1731. Three robbers had been hanged in the morning from the triple gallows known as the 'Three-Legged-Mare', but the bodies of Joseph Askwith and the brothers Richard and John Freeman had been cut down so as not to obscure the view of the punters. Monkey won easily in both heats, beating yet another horse called Brisk, bred by 'The Bloody-shouldered Arabian'.

So began the 258-year history of modern racing on the Knavesmire, interrupted only by the Kaiser and Adolf Hitler. Quite what the Fuehrer would have made of Dick Turpin can only be a matter of hypothesis, but a matter of fact is that Turpin did not make the celebrated ride to York, and there was no Black Bess.

The famous mare was a fiction of the balladeers, the pop singers of the time, and the ride was made sixty-three years before Dick Turpin met his maker on the Knavesmire on 20th August, 1739, a few hours before Smallhopes won the King's Plate, ridden by Thomas Turner.

Turpin was a small-time crook, brutal, uncouth and a rapist. He bore little resemblance to the man who really made the ride to York: the suave, elegant and debonair William 'Swift Nick' Nevison.

Nevison came from the Yorkshire town of Pontefract, and in June of 1676, this 'gentleman of the road' found himself at Gad's Hill, four miles from Gravesend, just as dawn was peeping over the Thames Estuary. The night's pickings had been lean, but Nevison snared a rich punter coming home with the milk. Mission accomplished, the highwayman rode to Gravesend, where he took a boat to ferry himself and his bay mare to Essex. He then rode on to Chelmsford, resting briefly before

galloping to Cambridge for a short halt and then moving to Huntingdon for some sleep and a fresh horse.

A relay of horses took Nevison up the Great North Road to York in time to bed down a weary animal, change his clothes and stroll to the bowling green to strike a bet with the Lord Mayor of York timed by that worthy at 7.45 p.m.

In due course, Nevison was charged and brought to trial, as he knew that he would be. The Lord Mayor was called as a witness and his

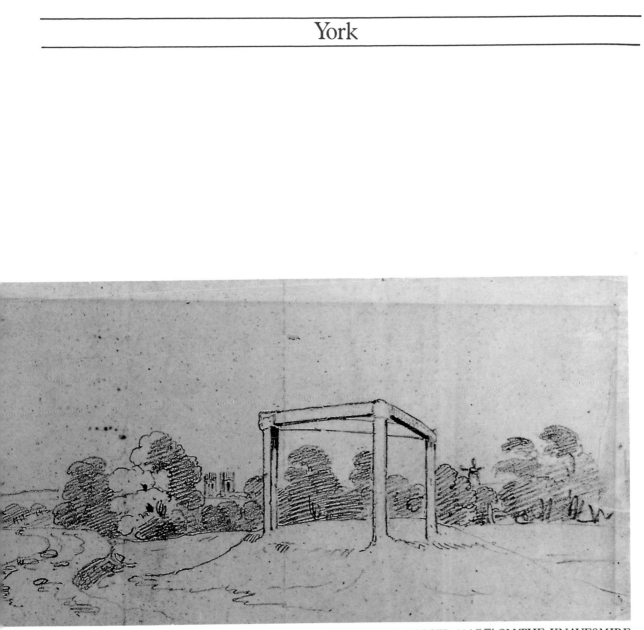

THE 'THREE-LEGGED-MARE' ON THE KNAVESMIRE

evidence was conclusive; the jury could not believe that a man could commit a crime in Kent and be in York, a journey of two hundred miles, on the same day.

Naturally, Nevison's charmed life could not last and he was convicted after shooting a man while trying to avoid capture. He was hanged on the Knavesmire in 1684, and the only other things he had in common with Dick Turpin were the leg irons they both wore in York Castle prison.

By 1751, York was the most important meet-ing in the North. The card included the King's Guineas, a Subscription Plate of £128 or upwards for five-year-olds over four miles and another Subscription Plate of £128 or upwards for four-year-old colts and fillies carrying 9st; this was to be run in two-mile heats. The City of York gave £50 to each race, and these two Subscription Races and the Jockey Club Plate at Newmarket were the most important races of the period.

At around this time the influence of Lord Rockingham, also the guiding light of Doncaster, became apparent. He commissioned the master mason John Carr to build a grandstand, financed by the issue of 250 £5 shares, entitling the shareholder to a free badge for the next hundred years; this was the period of the lease granted by the Corporation. The stand was opened on the morning of the summer meeting in 1755, following the execution of a murderer and a housebreaker. Patrons could enjoy the facilities of a refreshment room in the base of the stand, and watch the racing from either a 'great room' with a balustrade in front or the lead covered roof. It must have been a great improvement on the view from a carriage parked on the infield, although carriages were still parked on the inside rails near the finish as late as 1903.

The Gimcrack Club was formed in 1767 to commemorate the pony-sized grey horse who won twenty-six races from thirty-six starts in eleven years, including a walk-over, although Gimcrack was beaten in the only two races he contested at York. One of his defeats, the Great Subscription Race on Thursday, 6th August, 1768, was of some satisfaction to Lord Rockingham when the Marquis's Pilgrim, ridden by John Singleton Snr left Gimcrack well beaten in fifth and last place, although the little horse was conceding 7lb and two years in age.

The Club flourished, and the annual Gimcrack dinner at the racecourse is long established as a highlight of post-season celebrations. The owner of the winner of the Gimcrack Stakes for two-year-olds, founded in 1846, is the principal speaker, traditionally on the subject of racing politics.

The history of York is about as colourful as one could wish. There was a Royal racing scandal in 1791 when the Prince of Wales's jockey, Sam Chifney, was accused of cheating with the Prince's runners; probably true, since he did the same thing at Newmarket two months later and forced his Royal master's retirement from Headquarters.

In 1804, the Knavesmire was the backdrop to a story of intrigue, romance and jealousy worthy of the script of any soap opera. At this time women jockeys were few and far between, although in theory there was nothing to prevent them from race riding, and a ladies' race had been run at Ripon over fifty years before. Even so, Alicia Thornton was something different. She was the glamorous and sexy daughter of either a Norwich watchmaker or an Essex landowner, depending upon which account you prefer. She was either the live-in lover of Colonel Thomas Thornton, a gentleman who could trace his ancestry prior to the Conquest, or she was his legal wife; again the historians are at variance. One thing is certain: she was an absolute cracker, fair-haired and blue eyed, twenty-two years old and described as being as fascinating as Shakespeare's Merry Wives heroine Anne Page, but 'hardly of such pretty virginities'.

Riding in the park at Col. Thornton's seat, Thornville, Alicia and her brother-in-law, Captain Flint, decided on a match between their mounts. There was a little more to the match than the mere testing of thoroughbreds, as Flint was hopelessly in love with Alicia. She won this private race, and the gallant Captain challenged her to a race in public on the Knavesmire.

So it was that the two met again on 25th August, 1804. Attired in a fetching leopard-

ALICIA THORNTON'S MATCH AGAINST
MR FLINT

coloured jacket with blue sleeves and cap with a buff skirt concealing the pommel of her side-saddle, Alicia rode the Colonel's Vinagrillio out before a crowd of 100,000 spectators. It was four o'clock in the afternoon, and Flint steered Brown Thornville to the start escorted by the squadron of the 6th Light Dragoons, required to clear the course.

The stakes were £500 a side in bets and £1,000 to the winner. The betting was 5/1 on 'the petti-coat', but the odds shortened dramatically in running. Vinagrillio broke down inside the last mile of the four-mile catch-weight contest, and Brown Thornville cantered home alone.

Flint's aspirations to the heart of Alicia prob-ably foundered when he ordered her to keep to his left during the race, thus depriving her of the whip

hand, and cheerfully 'distanced' her when Vinagrillio went lame. Unlucky in love, lucky at cards! Alicia promptly issued a challenge for a return match, but this was thwarted when the jealous Colonel refused to settle on the first event.

Flint resorted to the conventional remedy of the time, and horsewhipped Thornton at the 1805 Summer meeting, only to find himself thrown into jail at a cost of £1,000 bail. Flint died of an overdose of prussic acid in 1832, and Thornton was even-tually forced to sell his estates, dying in France in 1823, although he won his case against Flint and was awarded 500 guineas damages in 1808.

Meanwhile, Alicia had wearied of fifty-three-year-old colonels and jealous lovers. Having been refused her revenge in a return match with Flint, she enhanced her reputation as the darling of the

Knavesmire by defeating no less than the Eddery of his day, Frank Buckle, in a match. Buckle rode Allegro and carried 13st 6lbs, Alicia put up 9st 6lb and ran out the head winner of the two-mile race, stunningly clad in purple cap and jacket with matching shoes. Buckle won twenty-seven classic races and had just ridden Meteora to victory in the 1805 Oaks. Even receiving four stone, Alicia's achievement riding side-saddle was remarkable. All things considered, she must have been quite a girl.

Most of York's luminaries lived in town houses in Micklegate, not roomy enough to accommodate large house parties. Accordingly, local inns prospered in race week without resorting to the modern practice of raising the price for the occasion.

The York Tavern, the leading hostelry in the city, was also the coaching inn, with a light coach leaving daily at 7 a.m., arriving with passengers and mail at noon in London the following day. The fare in 1789 was £2.10s inside, £1.15s outside, including fourteen pounds of luggage.

Most of the real action seems to have taken place at the Black Swan in Colney Street, known for licentious reasons as the Mucky Duck. Here a guinea or so a night could find you in the company of Prince Henry of the Netherlands, Lord Zetland, Lord Eglinton, the Duke of Roxburghe and if you were really unlucky, the Earl of Glasgow. The Earl did not enjoy the sweetest of tempers and thought little of throwing tardy waiters out of the window. When the management remonstrated, informing his lordship that the unfortunate man had broken an arm, the irascible peer said, 'Put him on the bill,' and was duly charged on his account 'breaking waiter's arm, £5'.

The Prince of Wales and his brother, the Duke of York, also stayed in lodgings, in Blake Street, when they came to see the Prince's 1788 Derby winner, Sir Thomas, win a 100 guineas sweepstake in 1789 before a huge crowd of Prinny's future subjects. That night, the royal party attended the local theatre and saw Elizabeth Farren, later to marry the 12th Earl of Derby, founder of the world's premier classic, play Beatrice in *Much Ado About Nothing*; apparently her performance received 'several marks of His Royal Highness's approbation'.

The late eighteenth and early nineteenth century management of York certainly did not lack imagination. In addition to the intrepid Alicia's races, in the spring of 1788 a match was staged between Mr Maynard on his unnamed bay mare, and Mr Baker on his grey horse, over a mile at level weights of thirty stone, which may account for the short distance, a veritable sprint by the standards of the time. Odds of 2/1 were laid on Mr Baker, but the mare won.

Yorkshire's senior courses, Doncaster and York, both grew up under differing styles of administration. Rockingham's patronage of Doncaster was controlled by the Corporation, and the Corporation still figure large today. York has always been run by a race committee, independent of the city for administration, but utterly dependent upon them for the lease of Knavesmire. The ridiculously frequent renewal required for the lease was to prove a stumbling block to York's security and progress to modernity, and a long-

ROWLANDSON'S 'TURFITES'

term solution was not found until as recently as 1962.

By 1839, the fortunes of the Knavesmire were at the lowest ebb since the abolition of public executions in 1801 halved the racecourse attendance. Only eight horses arrived for the Spring Meeting on 16th May, and the fixture was dropped. Lord Rockingham had long departed for the great stewards' room in the sky, there was no cup race and, horror of horrors, Hunt Club members on the Race Committee seemed to be organising the races. Something had to be done and the man to do it was John Orton, judge since 1830 and appointed Clerk of the Course in 1842.

Orton was a man of many parts. He was judge at no fewer than seven northern courses and all the tracks in Scotland. He was also a journalist for *The Sporting Magazine* and *The Yorkshireman* (a weekly sporting paper priced at fourpence ha'penny an issue or five shillings per quarter), and proprietor of the Turf Coffee House in York. He was also to prove to be a fine Turf historian and his *Turf Annals* of York and Doncaster, published in 1844, are a standard work upon which all researchers depend.

Experienced or not, his task was formidable. Doncaster, originally a poor relation, had become the North's premier track and the fortunes of York were not to be easily restored, but Orton's solution was simple: modernise the track and found a great race.

Realising the value of handicaps to the betting public, John Orton framed the Great Ebor Handicap over two miles, with stakes of £20, £15 forfeit, and £200 added money. Orton had judged

his market well and the victory of Pagan under 7st 13lb with Sim Templeman up, was the beginning of a new era for York, although Orton's track improvements incorporating a round course reduced the Ebor distance to a mile-and-three-quarters.

Orton replaced all wooden buildings with brick, railed in the back straight, laid down a lawn for the Members, and advised the stewards to instruct owners and trainers that no horse would be allowed to start at York without a prior examination of the animal's mouth by a veterinary surgeon.

This latter provision was necessary during the period known as the 'Filthy Forties' and followed the 1844 Derby victory of a ringer when 'Running Rein' turned out to be a four-year-old called Maccabaeus. Hence the examination of the length of the equine competitors' teeth.

The man who had exposed the Running Rein scandal was Lord George Bentinck, a man of great ability and high principle, but a vicious enemy. No-one seems to know how John Orton came to fall foul of Bentinck; perhaps it was something the latter had written in a sporting paper, perhaps Orton had judged a close race against a Bentinck runner when the money was down. In any event, Bentinck's influence as a senior member of the Jockey Club ensured Orton's dismissal. Broken-hearted, Orton's shabby treatment by the Race Committee forced him into retirement at his coffee house, where he died of drink on 19th May, 1845.

Timekeeping had by now become a problem, with frequent and irritating delays at the start. In August, 1866, it was announced 'the Clerk of the

GENERAL SCENES, 1890

VOLTIGEUR AND THE FLYING DUTCHMAN

Course at York will regulate his watch by the clock of York Cathedral, and will be fined five shillings for every minute he is behind in time in the bell ringing for the respective races'.

Joseph Lockwood was appointed Clerk, but the real administration of the course passed to a local steward, R.M. Jaques, a man much more of Bentinck's kidney. Jaques continued the work of revival started by Orton and founded the Gimcrack Stakes in 1846, a race for two-year-olds over one mile. The first winner was Ellerdale, owned by Admiral Harcourt, ridden by Tommy Lye, and trained by Tom Dawson Snr. at Middleham.

The Gimcrack became a six-furlong event in 1870, and together with the Ebor became a foundation stone of York's prestige in the modern day. The Gimcrack winners include Blink Bonny (Derby and Oaks winner in 1857), Sansovino (Derby winner in 1924), Bahram (who took the

Triple Crown in 1935), Black Tarquin (winner of the St Leger in 1948), Palestine (who won the Two Thousand Guineas in 1950) and Mill Reef, one of the finest Derby winners since the war. Nowadays, precocious breeding has eliminated the summer two-year-old races as classic pointers.

But to the betting man, nothing warms the heart like a handicap, and the Ebor's popularity amongst Yorkshire racing folk over the years has proved John Orton right. Some good horses have won, from The Hero, who triumphed in 1849 under 9st 4lb, having won two Ascot Gold Cups (then known as the Emperor's Plate) and the 1846 Doncaster Cup, to the tragic Kneller in 1988, who died unbeaten shortly afterwards with the world of long distance flat racing at his mercy. In between, Brown Jack won with 9st 5lb and his beloved Steve Donoghue in 1931. Another much-loved horse and jockey combination was cheered home by the

Knavesmire crowd in 1979 when Sea Pigeon and Jonjo O'Neill prevailed by a short head over Donegal Prince.

The Spring Meeting was revived in 1851. The star attraction was the finest match of all time, between Voltigeur and The Flying Dutchman. A huge crowd was expected at the Knavesmire on 13th May, and many walked the fifty miles from Cleveland to cheer on Lord Zetland's Voltigeur, winner of the Derby, Doncaster Cup and St Leger in 1850. His opponent, Lord Eglinton's The Flying Dutchman, was Derby and Leger winner in 1849. Voltigeur had beaten The Flying Dutchman in what became a match for the 1851 Doncaster Cup, having dead-heated with Russborough for the St Leger and won the run-off only two days before.

Horses certainly had to be tough in the mid-nineteenth century, since Voltigeur had raced five-and-three-quarter miles in forty-eight hours, and it is possible that The Flying Dutchman's Doncaster Cup defeat could be attributed to his jockey, Charles Marlow, who had been looking on the wine when it was red before the race. The drunken rider was no match for Nat Flatman, cool as ever a champion jockey should be, on Voltigeur.

An ashen-faced Eglinton, supporting his tearful jockey by now confessing all 'in vino veritas', proposed a return match. Lord Zetland accepted, and a £1,000 stake was the prize as Nat Flatman, riding at 8st on Voltigeur, cantered to the post at York alongside a sober Marlow who had weighed out with 8st 8lb 8oz for The Flying Dutchman. Admiral Rous, the Jockey Club handicapper, considered that the Dutchman should carry half a

ADMIRAL ROUS

pound more than weight for age and this was one of the few races (apart from give-and-takes) in which the weights were adjusted to a fraction.

As ever, Rous was not far out and The Flying Dutchman won by only a length, although many knowledgeable spectators reckoned that the issue was never in doubt. With the same mild eccentricity that applied to Gimcrack, The Great Voltigeur Stakes, founded in 1950 and a major St Leger trial, commemorates Voltigeur who never won a race at York.

It is hard to imagine National Hunt racing at

York

York, but bona-fide meetings took place on the Knavesmire from April 1867 to April 1885, inspired by the steeplechases organised to amuse the cavalry regiments quartered in the city. Shades of Severus; but racing on the Knavesmire in winter could not survive unless the horses had webbed feet, and the idea was sensibly abandoned.

The second half of the nineteenth century was dominated in York by two men: the jockey John Osborne and administrator James Melrose. Osborne won nine races for the Gimcrack Stakes between 1863 and 1880, and was known to the Knavesmire punters as 'The Bank of England', partly for his reputation for integrity and partly because he often outwitted the smart southern jockeys such as Archer, George Fordham and Tom Cannon. In 1869 he won the Derby on Pretender, the last northern-trained horse to win the premier classic at Epsom, and was still riding in 1892 at the age of fifty-nine.

James Melrose became Chairman of the York Race Committee in 1875. Sometime Lord Mayor, he laid the foundations of modern York, and his work was well done when he died at the age of 101 in 1929.

Two years earlier, Leslie Petch had been appointed auctioneer and judge, and a lifetime in racing brought him back to where he began, at York, as Clerk of the Course, when he relinquished the post of Senior Jockey Club judge in 1955.

The course had been a prisoner of war camp for six years during World War II before racing resumed on 4th September, 1945 with the substitute St Leger, run on the second day, won by Chamossaire and Tommy Lowrey before packed stands. The sheer size of the crowd defeated its own purpose; few could get a bet on and Chamossaire passed the line in silence and anti-climax.

Petch's job was essentially the same as Melrose's had been half a century or more before: to ensure the continuance of racing. In this he had an ally in the form of Charles, Earl of Halifax, a modern day Rockingham, and between them Petch and Halifax persuaded the city to grant a lease on the Knavesmire until 2056.

York flourished under Petch's management, and in 1965 new stands were opened by Lord Halifax. Ill health forced Petch to resign in 1971, but not before he had made the plans for a superb new race: the Benson and Hedges Gold Cup. This was a sponsored event for three-year-olds and upwards and run over the same distance as York's classic trial, the Dante Stakes, of one mile, two furlongs and 100 yards.

Leslie Petch's nephew, John Sanderson, succeeded him as Clerk of the Course and it was Sanderson who greeted Her Majesty the Queen on 15th August 1972 when she arrived for the three-day meeting and witnessed the inaugural running of the Benson and Hedges: the first monarch to grace York for 339 years.

The race was certainly a dish to set before a Queen. Only five ran, but they included Roberto, winner of the most controversial Derby since 1913. Ridden by Lester Piggott on that occasion, he'd won in a bumping match with Rheingold after Piggott had usurped the ride on Roberto from Bill Williamson in circumstances with which the racing public were soon to become familiar. The Panamanian Braulio Baeza had the ride on Roberto

JAMES MELROSE AND JOHN OSBORNE

in the Benson and Hedges, and Rheingold re-opposed on equal terms with Piggott in the saddle in place of his Derby jockey, Ernie Johnson.

The 3/1 on favourite was the mighty four-year-old Brigadier Gerard, perhaps the finest horse of his generation and unbeaten in fifteen races as he went to post under Joe Mercer. His triumphs included the Two Thousand Guineas (defeating Mill Reef), the Eclipse Stakes, the King George VI and Queen Elizabeth Stakes, and the Champion Stakes.

Gold Rod and Bright Beam completed the field in a race in which, in the words of *Raceform*, 'Roberto was out of the stalls like a bat out of hell', and made all to hold off Brigadier Gerard, who could never get on terms, by three lengths. Both first and second broke the course record and finished ten lengths clear of the third, Gold Rod.

Roberto's record stood for sixteen years until beaten by the subsequently disqualified Persian Heights, and the Benson and Hedges was quickly established as one of the top middle-distance races in Europe, with names such as Dahlia (1974 and '75), Wollow (1976), Troy (1979), Master Willie (1980), Commanche Run (1985) and Triptych

(1987) on the Roll of Honour.

The vagaries of commercial sponsorship resulted in a renaming of the race in 1986, when it became the Matchmaker International for two years. As I write it is known as the Judmonte International, worthy of its place as one of York's great races.

Outside the entrance to part of John Carr's grandstand, still there 234 years later and used as a champagne bar, there was until recently a flagstone measuring 6ft 4 inches by 3ft 6 inches. Two lines were cut into the stone, five feet apart and two feet in width. In the days when horses were handicapped according to height and age for the give-and-take races, the animals had to spread their feet out to the end of the two foot line before the height could be measured with a special calibrated stick. Hence the phrase – toe the line!

Let us leave York where we came in, with the Romans, and an unattributed quotation from that great enthusiast F.H. Bayles:

> *'Let Spain and Italy their climate boast,*
> *Britain shall ceaseless be our ardent toast,*
> *Of hoary York, that early throne of state,*
> *Where polished Romans sat in high debate.'* ■

YORK PANORAMA, 1981

CHEPSTOW

IN RECENT years, as the racing boom continues, it has become quite difficult to pick up and scan a sporting paper without reading of some enthusiastic entrepreneur announcing plans for the opening of a new racecourse in Britain, to say nothing of the proposals for all-weather tracks at existing venues.

Grays, in Essex, and Bournemouth have been the most recent suggestions, but as I write, Chepstow remains the newest course in the country, and that was opened over sixty years ago, in 1926.

This area of Wales, now in Gwent but formerly considered to be part of England and known for generations as Monmouthshire, is dominated by the magnificent ruins of Chepstow Castle, built in 1067 as a Norman fortress. Below the castle lies the pleasant market town of Chepstow, and to the north is Piercefield Park, a 400-acre site which is the home of flat racing in Wales.

Racing had taken place near Chepstow, at Parkwall, before 1772 and meetings were organised by the local hunt at Oakgrove in the mid-nineteenth century. By 1900, prize money totalled £1,850, but soon afterwards the Oakgrove meeting was abandoned, and it was twenty-six years before modern Chepstow, in spite of the inaccessibility of the course before the advent of motorways and the Severn Bridge, became a popular venue for trainers with animals of modest ability on the flat.

All this was in the future as the building gangs, led by a foreman rejoicing in the name of Hampshire Fats, sweated in the blistering heat of the summer of 1925; the deadline was 6th August, 1926, the date allocated by the Jockey Club for the first meeting.

Overcoming the difficulties of rock blasting and laying ashes for drainage, to be covered with beautiful turf taken from the centre of the Park to ensure good going from the outset, the building programme was on schedule until the General Strike brought the country to a standstill.

Fortunately, a week or so of unpaid idleness was enough for Hampshire Fats and his merry gang and they returned to their one shilling and sixpence (seven and a half new pence) an hour job at Piercefield. The job was completed by the end of

Chepstow

THE NEW COURSE, 1926

May at a cost of £150,000, but the celebrations were tinged with sadness. Hwfa Williams, the brains behind Sandown Park and the founder of the Eclipse Stakes, who had done much to ensure the successful launch of Chepstow, died before he could see his work at Piercefield Park come to fruition.

The first meeting went ahead on schedule and the entries were good, thirty-six horses travelling from Newmarket alone. The level of prize money on offer was superior to either Lewes or Thirsk, the

other meetings scheduled for 6th August, and most of the top jockeys were in attendance at Chepstow, colourfully described in the *Western Mail* as the 'Glorious Goodwood of the West'.

Amongst those thronging the weighing room were Brownie Carslake, Charlie Elliott, Freddy Fox, Henri Jelliss and Tommy Weston. Weston was to be champion jockey in 1926, in the conspicuous absence of Gordon Richards, who missed most of the season after contracting tuberculosis. However, Richards was to play a significant role in

Chepstow

Chepstow's history, as we shall see.

Special race trains from Bristol, Wolverhampton and West Wales brought most of the 20,000 racegoers, who were to see Henri Jelliss pilot Conca d'Oro to victory in the opening event, the £200 St Lawrence Selling Plate. Lord Glanely's appropriately named Chepstow Lass was second in this two-year-old contest. Glanely, a major shareholder and a steward of the meeting, promptly bought Conca d'Oro at the subsequent auction and went on to take the second race with Bucene, ridden by Joe Thwaites, perhaps best described as the Mark Birch of his day, and like Birch a fine ambassador for northern racing.

After Harry Cottrill's In Tune and Brownie Carslake had taken the last race of the day, the Monmouth Maiden Plate, the big crowd had some difficulty in getting away from the car parks. The irrepressible Lord Glanely, owner of 1919 Derby winner Grand Parade and known affectionately to racegoers as 'Old Guts and Gaiters', took personal charge in the middle of the road and directed the traffic for about an hour.

The second day was equally successful and despite the usual financial problems connected with such a venture, Chepstow was firmly on the racing map. The July Meeting the following season saw Chantrey, trained by Alec Taylor and ridden by course specialist Henri Jelliss win the first running of the Welsh Derby. The next day the same trainer and jockey combination won the Welsh Oaks with Book Law, on her way to victory in the St Leger at Doncaster.

A Welsh St Leger was run in September, and again Alec Taylor had the winner with Sledmere.

Taylor retired at the end of 1927, doubtless to the relief of his rivals.

The attention of the racing world was focused again on Chepstow in the Autumn of 1933. Gordon 'Moppy' Richards, now happily restored to health and already the winner of six of his ultimate twenty-six championships, won the fifth race at Nottingham on 3rd October, The Elvaston Plate, on a horse called Barnby. Popular mythology has it that the Elvaston Plate was the last race on the Nottingham card, but in fact Michael Beary on Nitsichin won the final event and Richards did not have a ride.

The following day, Richards went through the card at Chepstow. As ever, all the top jockeys were riding, including Weston, Carslake, Dick Perryman and 'Midge' Richardson, but the Four Horsemen of the Apocalypse wouldn't have stopped Gordon in such superb form.

Richards won the opening race on the second day, and the next. Arriving at the start for the third, Fred Herbert, a jockey who went on riding into his sixties and was known as 'Brusher' because of his pacemaking style acquired on the training grounds in flat-out 'brushing' gallops, jokingly appealed to the starter, 'We can't beat Gordon, so you'll have to help us!'.

Not unnaturally, the starter declined to assist and Gordon went on to win that race and the next two. He had now set a record of twelve consecutive winners, but in the last he went under by a head and a neck, giving the winner, Lament, thirty-four pounds including future champion Doug Smith's five pound apprentice allowance.

So, history was made at Chepstow. Delighted

punters swarmed around the weighing room and their pint-sized hero led them as they sang 'Little Man, You've Had a Busy Day'. He certainly had.

Richards's record was to stand for twenty-five years until the Rhodesian jockey Pieter Stroebel matched the twelve-winner sequence at Bulawayo in 1958.

Chepstow has continued to provide modest but essential opportunities for flat race horses in beautiful surroundings and is deservedly popular, although nowadays it is better known as a National Hunt course and the home of the Welsh Grand National.

The early days of Chepstow were guided by Henry Hyde, for many years supremo of his family's course at Kempton Park, but the post-war prosperity of the Welsh course is chiefly due to the magnificent entrepreneurial skills of the late John Hughes, the man who restored Aintree to Grand National glory and whose untimely death in 1988 deprived racing of the services of the finest racecourse manager in the past thirty years. ■

LORD GLANELY AND GORDON RICHARDS, 1930

CHESTER

THE ANCIENT city of Chester was founded nearly 2,000 years ago by the Romans. If racing took place then and there, it is not recorded and although it is likely that, as at York, the Roman soldiers and civil servants ran horse races to amuse the garrison, the earliest date that bears any credence is 1511, when one Reverend Robert Rogers records 'running of horses' amongst other sports on the Rood Eye, in the third year of the reign of Henry VIII.

The Rood Eye, or Roodee as it became known, was originally the island of the Rood or Cross. An order of the Corporation of Chester dated 10th January, 1511 decrees that a silver ball, of an annual value of three shillings and fourpence, 'the reward of speedy runnings', should in future always be run for by horses on a course on the Rood Eye.

It is interesting to note that the prize of a silver ball superseded a wooden ball, originally awarded for foot racing, but the good citizens of Chester grew weary of being cheated by the 'talking horses', i.e. the pedestrian sportsmen. The punters sensibly preferred dumb beasts and thus coined the adage 'never bet on anything that talks'.

The Silver Ball was still going strong in 1540 and the races took place on Shrove Tuesday, little seeming to alter until 1609 when the date was changed to St George's Day and the race was re-named the St George's Race. This move reflected an early form of sponsorship as Robert Amery, an ironmonger and former Sheriff of Chester, gave three bells for the first three home, and fixed the distance as 'from the New Tower to the Netes'.

These were challenge bells, and security had to be given for their safe return in time for the next season. However the winners appeared to have divided the entrance fees, thus pioneering the idea of the sweepstake that we know today as a fundamental part of the prize-money system. Quite why St George's Day, the 23rd April, was decided upon for the race, no-one seems to know; perhaps the wise Cestrians did not wish their race meeting to be subject to the movable feast of Easter as opposed to a fixed, and firm, date.

1624 saw further changes in the conditions of the race. The Mayor of Chester, an innkeeper called John Brereton, decided that the Bell, by this time paid for by the Corporation and worth 'eight or ten pounds' should become the exclusive property of the winner, but that the race should start beyond the New Tower and be run five times round the Roodeye.

The race thus became a five-mile event, run in heats, and even at catch-weights it is not surprising to find that local chroniclers reckoned that the race would get to the bottom of any thirteen and a half hands horse, the general type and size of racing animals during this period.

However, by 1665 times were hard. The Civil War and eleven years of Cromwellian rule had left the gentry short of cash and they found themselves unable to support the races, but help was at hand. Not for the last time in racing history, the Derby family stepped into the breach and the eighth Earl announced in the *London Gazette* that he, together with 'many other Gentlemen of Quality within the two Counties of Lancaster and Chester and the Mayor, Aldermen and Burgesses of Liverpool, have set forth near the said Town a five mile

THE ROODEE, 1890

Course for a Horse Race to be run on the 18th March next, and so for ever yearly at the same time.'

Lord Derby went on to leave no room for doubt that a very decent Plate would be on offer, doubtless funded by his Lordship in the event of a poor entry. All went well, and the race which was to be the forerunner of the centrepiece of modern Chester, the Chester Cup, was in safe hands.

1683 has claims of a royal jockey winning a race at Chester. James, Duke of Monmouth and illegitimate son of King Charles II and Lucy Walter, was reckoned by Scarth Dixon, writing under the nom-de-plume of 'The British Yeoman' in the 'Pink Un', to have won the 'Chester Cup' on his own horse. It is more probable that the thirty-four-year-old Duke rode his winner at nearby Wallasey, considered to be more of a course for gentlemen. At all events, his pleasure must have been short-lived as this was the year of the Rye House Plot in which the Duke was implicated.

Rye House was at Hoddesdon in Hertfordshire and lay at a conveniently narrow point on the Newmarket Road, ideal for the assassination of his father, the King, and Monmouth's rival to the throne, the Duke of York, as they returned from the races on 22nd March, 1683.

The plot failed as a fire at his lodgings caused the King and his brother to retreat to London earlier than expected. Monmouth was later betrayed and exiled to the Continent, albeit with an annuity of £6,000 a year.

All of which goes to prove the affinity between racing and royalty. Chester's racing continued to prosper during the next three reigns, although sad to relate, royal jockey Monmouth had his head chopped off on Tower Hill after attempting a feeble rebellion.

Chester Races as an organised meeting figure for the first time in the record books for 1729. By now we are back to late April, the 22nd in fact, and Mr Williams-Wynn's chestnut mare Trusty Kate won the Give and Take Plate (a handicap with the weights decided by size rather than ability) after four heats, and Sir N. Curzon's Bravo took the £30 Plate for five-year-olds after only two heats.

In 1741, Sir Richard Grosvenor of the family who were to play a large part in the preservation of Chester, donated a £50 gold cup for a race for six-year-olds carrying 11st. This welter event was won by that equine rarity, a black horse, owned by Mr Pulleyne and bearing the unhappy name of Sloven. The same animal won the City Plate, as Lord Derby's 1665 race was now known, in 1743.

The meeting was moved to May in 1758, when a five-day festival was held. It is common today for the Chester Cup to be the happy hunting ground of punters' old friends; the names of Trelawny, Major Rose, Attivo, John Cherry, Donegal Prince and Sea Pigeon come to mind.

The first of this distinguished line of equine objects of human affection was Statesman, winner of the Chester City Plate in 1765, 1766 and 1767. In 1765 he was described as 'aged', i.e. more than six years old, but he had no difficulty in disposing of top-class younger rivals, including Speedwell, in three successive years, and rounded off on the final day of the 1767 meeting by winning the £5 Give and Take Plate under 9st 9lb 10oz after humping 10st to victory in the City Plate. Statesman did not contest the City Plate in 1768, but again he was a good thing for the Give and Take, carrying fourteen ounces less.

Over the years, Chester had flirted with the idea of an autumn meeting, the last of these being held in 1768. Under the patronage of Lord Grosvenor, founder of the Eaton Stud at his family seat of nearby Eaton Hall and destined to own eight classic winners, the card was revived in 1774 and included a Grosvenor Gold Cup of £50, switched from the spring meeting. This was won by Mr Norcrop's Intrepid, although his Lordship did not go away empty-handed either, as his Stephano took the other principal race of the day.

The following year Lord Grosvenor was again successful at the September meeting with the gallant Stephano as well as Rustic and India. But winning his own money back still proved elusive; the Gold Cup was won by the curiously named 'Mine-Ass-in-a-Band Box' – a nomenclature which might have trouble passing the scrutiny of Messrs Weatherby today.

Lord Grosvenor riposted with an animal by Match'em, neatly named Short-Hose, and won his own Cup in 1776, but although better fields were being attracted, the autumn racing was again abandoned in 1782 and the Grosvenor Cup returned to the spring meeting.

As early as 1796, modern Chester was taking shape with the class horse of his day, a four-year-old colt by Young Marske, collecting both the City Plate and the Grosvenor Gold Cup. However, in

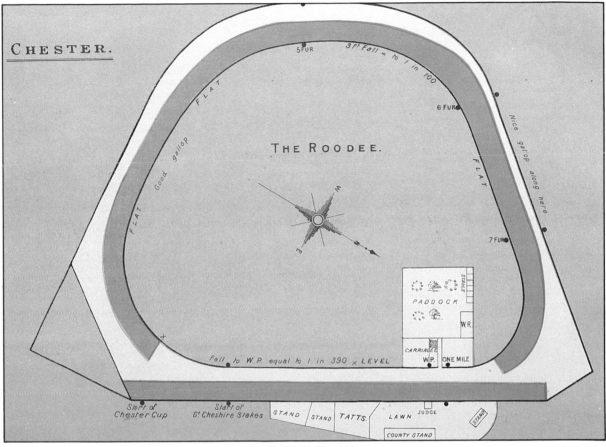

THE COURSE, 1903

order to do so, he had to run twenty-two miles, as the events were a course of heats. In 1820, Sultan had to complete twenty miles at racing pace on 8th May to secure the City Plate and the Gold Cup. Some other race meetings had already placed on their programmes a series of single races as the tough, needless and exhausting process of heat racing fell out of vogue.

At the turn of the century, these single races were well established; in 1801 the Grosvenor Cup was a silver trophy, won by Pilgrim. In 1802 the feature races at the meeting were the long-distance City Plate, popular since 1729, and the more recent Earl of Chester's Plate, both over three miles.

The City Plate had evolved from the silver ball of King Henry's day, to the St George's race saved by Lord Derby and was to survive for another thirty-three years until the Municipal Capitals

Reform Act made it illegal to provide prize money out of public funds. But it was the innovation of single races over varying distances which was increasing the popularity of Chester at the expense of other principal meetings such as York and Epsom, where the running was often confined to heats and one race could take all day.

The enjoyment of Chester racegoers at this time was enhanced by the exploits of a remarkable horse called Cheshire Cheese, originally named Belisle.

Cheshire Cheese had achieved little on the racecourse and had been sent to stud at Knutsford in Cheshire. The change of air and perhaps the congenial duties at stud worked wonders and the horse was put back into training.

In 1803 Cheshire Cheese won a Fifteen Guineas Sweepstakes for maidens over two miles, on the

Chester

first day of the meeting, and followed up by taking the Earl of Chester's Plate under 9st on the next day, adding 100 guineas to the winnings on behalf of his owner Mr Charles Cholmondeley. On the third day he enjoyed an easy victory in a twenty sovereign stakes race over two miles, and Mr Cholmondeley left Chester races £345 the richer all told with bets included.

That season, Cheshire Cheese also cleaned up in Royal Plates at Newcastle and Lichfield, and was something of a popular hero when he made his debut the following year at Catterick on 5th April, easily winning the Macaroni Stakes worth 150 sovereigns and ridden by his owner at 12st 7lbs.

The run came to an end when Cheshire Cheese failed to give 18lbs to Lord Stamford's Sir Oliver in the Earl of Chester's Plate on 30th April but his many supporters got their money back with interest when he won the City Plate the next day. Mr Cholmondeley then went pot-hunting with his popular six-year-old, and after winning a £70 race at Nantwich, Cholmondeley was offered 10 guineas by the Clerk of the Course to withdraw Cheshire Cheese from the following day's £50 Plate. Almost unbeatable in Cheshire, the horse found things too hot for him when venturing further south, and was trounced by the Prince of Wales's Aniseed at Bibury.

In passing, it seems that Mr Cholmondeley had a penchant for epicurean names; another of his horses rejoiced in the name of Welsh Rabbit, although it was not a unique predilection, as one of the most successful animals of the period, a son of Whiskey, was called Sir Ulic Mackilligut.

The Grosvenor Stakes was first run in 1819

and in 1824 the Tradesmen's Cup, later to become the Chester Cup, was inaugurated with 100 guineas added to the fifteen guineas handicap sweepstake. Twenty-four subscribed with seven final acceptors for the race, run on 3rd May, 'twice round the roodee'.

Victory went to the Doge of Venice, sired by Sir Oliver, who had lowered Cheshire Cheese's colours in the Earl of Chester's Plate twenty-one years earlier. The six-year-old was ridden by T. Nicholson at 9st 2lb and started 6/4 favourite, but the handicap was limited, with the lowest weight 8st 2lb.

The Dee Stakes had joined the Calendar in 1819 and since 1775, the Chester meetings had attracted all the great names of northern society, with brilliant gatherings at the Assembly Rooms in the evenings, and concerts of 'music and bells' for the ladies, while the gentlemen amused themselves at the cock-fights taking place at any of the 140 inns and public houses in the city.

The Tradesmen's, or Chester Cup, soon waxed high in popularity, especially when wider handicapping came into practice and the weight range attracted gambling on a huge scale. Soon the Cup was a heavier betting race than the Derby, and attracted entries from all over the country – inspiring an ante-post market that would last, in the words of one reporter, 'through the winter and right to flag fall'.

Inevitably, local sportsmen found it hard to compete with the fat cats looking for a good touch, but one or two managed to hold their own and with interest. The name of Jack Mytton stands out, a man who bet fearlessly and, starting with a bottle

100

of wine while shaving, consumed six bottles of port daily.

Succeeding in being expelled from both Harrow and Winchester, a neat double if ever I heard of one, Mytton served in the 7th Hussars in the Army of Occupation in France following Waterloo, contriving to lose 16,000 Napoleons in a bent billiard match. This sportsman, who really deserves a book to himself, took thousands out of the ring when Halston, named after his Shropshire estate, won the Chester Cup cleverly under 8st in 1829. Five years later Mytton lay dead in the Fleet debtors' prison.

The Old City Plate, or St George's race, was run for the last time in 1835, but these were vintage years for Chester. Old Sam Darling, progenitor of a great racing family and successful on Rockingham in the 1833 St Leger, won the Cup in the same year on Pickpocket, and again on Lord Westminster's Cardinal Puff in 1839, with a steadier of 9st 3lb. Nat Flatman, champion jockey from 1846 to 1852, scored in 1840 on The Dey of Algiers carrying 7st 10lb, but by this time Chester's popularity was attracting very large fields. Twenty runners contested the 1840 race, a few too many for the tight circuit in Flatman's view and like Fred Archer thirty-five years later, he hated the place; The Dey of Algiers was his only Cup winner.

Alice Hawthorne, a superb racemare who won fifty-two races in seven seasons, landed a gamble in the Cup of 1842 when chucked in with only 6st, but her backers burnt their fingers in 1844 when she attempted to give 5st 8lb to Red Deer, the first three-year-old to win the Chester Cup.

This famous coup, engineered by Lord George Bentinck, at that time managing the horses of the Duke of Richmond, is said to have netted £100,000 in bets for Bentinck and despite several false starts, the result was never in doubt, Red Deer making all to win by 'about fifty lengths'.

Alice Hawthorne was second of the twenty-six runners, and must have been rounding the turn for home as Red Deer went past the post. His diminutive jockey, Kitchener, took another half circuit to pull up, but this is not surprising as Red Deer carried only 4st and Kitchener weighed 3st 4lb. At Ascot in 1840, he had ridden in the Wokingham Stakes when weighing only 2st 3lb, so by Chester the lad was positively corpulent.

Not that such weights were unusual at this time; George Fordham, who was to be champion jockey fifteen times, weighed 3st 10lb when he started riding and won the 1854 Chester Cup on Epaminodas carrying 4st 10lb.

The fields were not getting any smaller, however, and in 1852 a record forty-three horses accepted for the Chester Cup. The mandatory draw for places at the start, familiar on all courses today, was many years in the future, but Chester's narrow conformation demanded a draw in the interests of safety, and the field lined up in two ranks, with the eventual winner Joe Miller drawn ten of the twenty-two runners in the front rank.

Joe Miller made all under 4st 10lb in the hands of Jim Goater to land the stakes of £2,870 and some substantial ante-post bets at all odds from 24/1. Stilton finished second (it seems impossible to get away from cheese at Chester) but Joe Miller must have been something of a good thing, as he went on to win the Ascot Gold Cup, temporarily known as

the Emperor's Plate, from a useful field including the great Voltigeur, the Derby and Leger winner of 1850.

We cannot leave the 1850s without reference to the race for the Cup in 1853. The 3/1 favourite was Trifle, ridden by John 'Tiny' Wells for the Wantage gambling trainer Tom Parr, and would probably have won but for having a barging match with Talfourd as the twenty-eight strong field negotiated the final circuit. The rank outsider Goldfinder came through to win by half a neck from Talfourd with Trifle back in third.

Goldfinder was owned by Dr William Palmer, who won £3,000 in stakes and took £12,000 out of the ring. Palmer was later unmasked as a poisoner and clearly gave illicit medication to his horses as well as his patients. His filly Nettle, purchased with the insurance payment obtained by the murder of his wife, bolted wildly during the race for the Oaks in 1855, breaking the leg of her jockey, Marlow. No-one was quite sure who had been got at, the jockey or the horse, but Palmer was hanged at Stafford the following year for poisoning his closest friend, John Parsons Cook.

However, in the 1860s, shadows of suspicion started to lengthen over the Roodee. It was suggested in some sections of the press that the handicap for the Cup was becoming too easy meat for the landing of a gamble and the Race Committee decided that the handicapper, Mr Edward Topham, should submit his work to the Stewards of the Jockey Club prior to publication of the weights.

Matters were not helped by memories of 1859, when the huge fields on the soup plate of a course

CHESTER VIEWS IN 1933 (MAIN PICTURE) AND 1977

resulted in the inevitable accident. A horse was killed and three jockeys, including Tiny Wells, were injured. Wells recovered in time to ride Musjid to victory in the Derby, but Chester was undoubtedly losing popularity. In 1873 it was suggested that the meeting, now a four-day affair, be reduced to three. In the same year Mr Edward Topham, who had been Clerk of the Course and handicapper for over thirty years, died and was succeeded by his son Joseph Topham, but he was unable to halt the steady decline, which was both sporting and social.

There were a few highlights and Fred Archer defied his dislike of the track by riding nine winners at the 1881 meeting. But the 1885 gathering was described in a local paper as the worst meeting ever held on the Roodee, the quality of the runners having sunk to an all-time low.

Things had improved by 1893, when the Tradesmen's Cup was run as the Chester Cup for the first time and the course properly enclosed with an entrance fee to the public.

This was the work of a new Clerk of the Course, R.K. Mainwaring, who was to play a major part in Chester's revival with strong support from the Grosvenor family in the dignified form of the First Duke of Westminster, reputedly the richest man in England and breeder of two Triple Crown winners at Eaton Hall.

In 1894 the prize for the Chester Cup included a Cheshire cheese for the first time, thus continuing the culinary theme set by Cholmondeley's course specialist back in 1803. The innovation was a great success and John Corlett, editor of the *Pink Un* eulogised about the cheese in his sporting

FRED ARCHER

paper. Bad jokes abounded, one correspondent declaring that although the cheese wouldn't last long, it certainly brought flavour to the race.

But more serious matters were afoot. Mainwaring and his aristocratic patron embarked on a programme of modernisation to restore Chester to its former glory. By the time the Prince of Wales, later King Edward VII made his first visit to Chester in 1899, thus putting £1,500 on the gate, plans were well in hand for replacement of the old uncovered single-deck stands at a cost of £12,000 and the Chester card could boast more added money than any racecourse in the country, except Ascot.

Sadly, the Duke of Westminster could not achieve his ambition to win the Chester Cup in what was to be the last year of his life. It would have been poetic justice if his runner, Batt, had prevailed, but Batt could do no better than second to Uncle Mac, giving seven pounds. A patrician of the old school, the Duke at least had the satisfaction of having done much to preserve the course that his ancestors had loved; and Batt was to play his part in racing history, as we shall see.

The new century opened quietly. The death of the Duke and the war in South Africa put racegoers in a sombre mood, and only a modest crowd assembled to try the new covered grandstands and to witness Tod Sloan taking the Cup by three lengths on Roughside in 1900.

However, by 1903 the new Duke of Westminster was entertaining in the County Stand, and all the Lancastrian fancy and fashion were turned out in force. The draw for places at the start was now mandatory and 'the luck of the draw' became a

DUKE OF WESTMINSTER, 1899

matter for much press comment. It had mattered little when jockeys rode with an upright seat and the racing pace was much slower, but Tod Sloan changed all that with his 'Monkey up a Stick' crouch style. At Chester, an inside draw on the tight left-handed track was soon considered imperative.

Nonetheless, 'pole position' could prove a mixed blessing if the horse did not have the pace or the jockey did not have the skill to maintain the place on the rails, and many an animal used up so much energy that there was nothing left to fight out a finish. Even so the mythology continues to this day, despite *Timeform*'s view that 'the draw is of little consequence', adding the rider that 'a slow start is virtually impossible to overcome in sprint races'.

In 1907 the Chester Vase was inaugurated and resulted in a dead heat between Sancy and Earlston. The stakes were divided and Sancy's owner, Sir William Bass, won the Vase after a toss-up.

The meeting of 1915 was the last for four years as Britain plunged into the First World War, and the Cup was won by Steve Donoghue on Hare Hill. Donoghue was already champion jockey, and a brilliant career lay before him, but he was always to maintain that winning the Chester Cup was worth more to him than all his classic victories. As a ragged fourteen-year-old playing truant from his school in Warrington, Donoghue trudged twenty-one miles to Chester to seek out John Porter, the Duke of Westminster's trainer, and begged for a job in his stables.

Porter took the boy on, subject to his father's approval, and Donoghue scampered off to the races and sat on the city wall to watch Big Mac defeat Batt in the Cup. Resolving that he would one day ride the Cup winner, Donoghue started his racing career by accompanying Batt back to Porter's Berkshire stable.

Racing resumed in 1919 before the usual gratuity-happy post-war crowds. Nearly 81,000 people paid £19,438 in the hope of seeing the appropriately named Air Raid win the Chester Cup under 9st 8lb. Air Raid had won the Chester Vase with 9st 8lb on the opening day and went to post 5/2 favourite for the Cup. Much of the ex-servicemen's cash must have ended in the bookies' satchels; Air Raid could only finish third.

The stands built in eight months in the summer of 1899 were to remain for eighty-five years until they were destroyed by fire in the early hours of the morning of 28th September, 1985, and with the exception of the war period of 1940 to 1945, bore witness to more than one epic equine contest and saw not a few equine heroes including Brown Jack, Chester Cup winner in 1931, as well as those already listed above.

Although the course does not resemble Epsom in any way, except that it is left-handed, the tight turns of Chester make it an ideal test of the adaptability required for the Derby. Papyrus, Hyperion, Windsor Lad, Henbit and Shergar all won the Chester Vase over the full Derby distance before going on to victory at Epsom, and Parthia took the Dee Stakes over the same trip prior to his triumph in the world's premier classic.

The Ormonde Stakes, originally a five-furlong two-year-old event, was first run over the present distance of one mile, five furlongs and seventy-five yards in 1936, and probably there has never been a better contest. Quashed, one of the gamest mares ever seen on a racecourse and later to defeat the American Triple Crown winner Omaha in the Ascot Gold Cup, beat another top-class stayer, Cecil, by a neck after a desperately hard race. Although usually won by older horses, the Ormonde indicated the talents of Derby winner Tulyar in 1952.

In 1988, the fire-ravaged stands were rebuilt at a cost of £3,000,000 although racing had continued in 1986 and 1987. All racecourses are unique, insofar as they are all different, but to paraphrase George Orwell, one is more unique than others: and that course is Chester. ∎

CHESTER CUP DAY ON THE 'SOUP-PLATE'
COURSE, 1923

HAYDOCK

WITH THE old and once famous course at Castle Irwell, where the flat season used to come to its bitter end in Manchester's mid-November gloom, closed since 1963, and Liverpool now devoted to National Hunt racing, only Haydock Park remains to fly a lone flag for flat racing in the County Palatine once known as Lancashire.

Racing in the area was first recorded at Golborne Heath in 1752 when a £50 Cup was competed for on 16th June, sponsored by the Newton Hunt, for horses owned by members 'not in the Sweats', i.e. not in training before 1st March.

By 1807, racing was taking place at Newton-le-Willows and a four-mile one hundred guineas Newton Gold Cup was founded in the same year that the Prince of Wales presided over the inaugural running of the Ascot Gold Cup with identical conditions. The track, which was on common ground about two miles from the present course at Haydock, attracted some good horses and the top northern jockeys were not ashamed to 'farm' the events at the May three-day meeting when the southern-based riders were busy at Newmarket. The contrasting characters of Jim Snowden and Johnny Osborne were to be found well to the fore.

The final event at Newton Common was in July, 1898. The following year, the 127-acre park at Haydock was leased from Lord Newton, and a National Hunt meeting was staged on 10th February. On 12th May, Fred Rickaby steered Beatitude into the winner's circle after victory in the appropriately named Golborne Stakes, a five-furlong race for two-year-olds.

The Newton Cup was now a mile-and-a-quarter handicap, having been a three-mile race in 1825, and contested over a mile and a half in the late nineteenth century, reduced to one mile in 1898. Today, Haydock's oldest established race is again a mile-and-a-half affair, worth £17,000 in 1988.

By way of contrast, the Ascot Gold Cup was worth nearly £70,000, but the comparison is only academic as the races that started so similarly now differ so widely.

With the nearby Liverpool Docks playing a massive supporting role in the submarine war for the Western Approaches, racing was impossible until Adolf had bitten on the cyanide pill and peace returned to Europe. On 14th August, 1946, Haydock re-opened and the course steadily built a reputation for good-class racing, with the public and the horses alike enjoying the pleasures of the tree-shaded paddock.

In 1948, Lord Derby's Swallow Tail won the six-furlong Bettisfield Plate and went on to be a desperately unlucky third in the Derby the following year, the victim of a not-so-gentle spot of gamesmanship by winning jockey Charlie Elliott on Nimbus.

The Lancashire Oaks, founded at Manchester in 1939 and transferred to Haydock in 1963, the John of Gaunt Stakes, a seven-furlong race named after Shakespeare's 'time-honour'd Lancaster', the Old Newton Cup and the quaintly named Buggins Farm Nursery all sustain Haydock's traditions, but the one to beat the band is the Vernons Sprint Cup.

Nowadays run in September to avoid the mists

Haydock Park

and mellow fruitfulness which caused abandonment in 1968 and the late season heavy ground which often took the essential spring out of a sprint race, the event was founded in 1966 as the Vernons November Sprint Cup for two-year-olds and upwards. Peter O'Sullevan's Be Friendly won the inaugural race as a juvenile in the hands of the apprentice Colin Williams, and again in 1967 piloted by Scobie Breasley.

Be Friendly's 1966 victory was worth £5,337 5s to the winner, in contrast to the £85,590 value when Dowsing won a now Group One race in 1988.

Until 1986, tactics were all important as the six-furlong course started on a chute with a sharp left-hand turn into the straight with half a mile still to run; while this in theory gave the advantage to horses with a low draw, the ground on the stands side in wet weather nullified the inside track and many runners sacrificed lengths by crossing at the bend. In recent years a straight six has made the racing fair, if a little less interesting.

As I write, the stands built in 1899 are being demolished to make way for a new grandstand complex at a cost of two million pounds, to be opened in 1990. This would have pleased the late Sydney Sandon, who became Secretary in 1908 and later Chairman and Managing Director. The Sydney Sandon Stakes, a mile race for three-year-olds, commemorates the man who did much to make Haydock a worthy survivor of the traditions of Lancastrian racing. ■

LEICESTER

As WOULD be expected from a location in the heart of England's hunting country, racing in the Leicester area predates the Stuarts, although possibly by only a day, racing being recorded on 23rd March, 1603, the day before the death of Queen Elizabeth I and the succession of 'our cousin of Scotland', James I.

The earliest known venue was at Abbey Meadow, under the patronage of the Earl of Rutland, who donated an Earl of Rutland's Plate in 1690 while the Mayor dispensed hospitality to the tune of £1. 14s. for the entertainment of a Colonel Lister and several of that gallant officer's thirsty friends anxious for a little 'wyne and ale'.

As a gallon of sack cost about six shillings, doubtless a merry time was had by all, including the civic authorities who gave a £2 Town Plate. By 1720, this prize was boosted by a compulsory donation of one shilling by each of the twenty-four aldermen; the councillors, of whom there were forty-eight, getting away with sixpence each.

Seventy-two people were therefore governing the City of Leicester in the early eighteenth century, not including the Mayor, but this early example of Parkinson's Law did not prevent them from continuing to boost prize money from the civic purse. By the 1740s, as the meeting transferred to St Mary's Field, a local entrepreneur, by the name of Langton, was hiring the Town Hall to accommodate the gentry and their ladies visiting the races.

By the turn of the century, the meeting could be described as 'an annual festival', but not everyone was happy with that and there were the usual objections on moral grounds. The venue had to be changed yet again, and in 1806 moved to Victoria Park, with the Duke of Rutland giving twenty guineas added money to the Belvoir Stakes.

By 1840, a two-day meeting was well established in September, the prizes including a 100 sovereign Gold Cup, first introduced in 1807, and a Queen's Plate of 100 sovereigns, plus 'several valuable stakes'. The local theatre, described as 'a neat building' by James Whyte, was open during the races and the cognoscenti could disport themselves in a suite of assembly rooms designed as a hotel and generally used as Judge's Lodgings during the assizes.

The meeting continued to prosper, but in 1883 the Jockey Club took the view that the Victoria Park course was 'a very unsuitable one for racing'. Despite a petition signed by 11,000 punters and presented to the Club by the Duke of Rutland, Victoria Park had to close and a new track was found at Oadby, the present site.

The course was designed and laid out on farmland by Tom Cannon who was later to become Clerk of the Course at Stockbridge on retirement from a career which included thirteen classic winners as a jockey and two as a trainer, while inadvertently becoming Lester Piggott's great-grandfather.

In spite of impeccable antecedents, Oadby did not do well. Even today, the course would not win prizes in the most agricultural of beauty contests, and clearly lacked the charm of Victoria Park. The fashion and the fancy disappeared but the course survived the lack of patronage to become what is best described as a bread-and-butter course, with good-sized fields and competitive racing. Tom

TOM CANNON

Cannon had the forethought to provide a straight mile, which makes Leicester almost unique among the minor courses and attractive to trainers who also find the geographical location in the Midlands handy for most training centres.

Leicester was to provide the backdrop to the early exploits of two Turf champions in very different fields; one was human, the other equine. On 31st March, 1921, Gordon Richards scored the first of 4,870 winners on Gay Lord; last of the six runners was an animal with the unhappy name of Toilet, and clearly destined to go down the pan.

But perhaps Leicester's chief claim to fame lies not in the world of flat racing, but 'over the sticks'. A dual-purpose track, it was the scene of Golden Miller's first victory in a hurdle race in 1931. Comparing the giants of different generations has always been a popular sporting pastime, if an inconclusive one, but Golden Miller was the Desert Orchid of the day.

It is interesting to speculate how many Leicester racegoers knew they were in the presence of one of the great champions of the future on the 20th January, 1931 as Golden Miller hacked up in the Gopsall Maiden Hurdle, ridden by Bob Lyall.

ROWLEY MILE

JULY COURSE

NEWMARKET

'In days of ease, when now the weary sword
Was sheath'd, and luxury with Charles
*   restor'd . . .*
The Peers grew proud in horsemanship t'excel,
Newmarket's glory rose, as Britain's fell . . .'
                                    Alexander Pope
                        (in a worse mood than usual)

NOT MANY years after the death of Christ, Queen Boadicea of the Iceni founded a royal stud at Exning in Suffolk. She financed the enterprise, which was to export British-bred horses to Rome, with money borrowed from the Roman philosopher, Seneca.

In the year AD 60, on the death of Boadicea's husband, Prasutagus, the King of Norfolk and Suffolk, Seneca called in the loan. Boadicea refused to pay, incurring the wrath of the Roman tax-colleetors and bailiffs who flogged the Queen and raped her two daughters. In revenge Boadicea raised the Iceni in rebellion, savaging the Romans at Colchester, St Albans and London before, like many a good punter since, coming to grief at Towcester.

Unable to face capture, the Queen took poison. To her eternal memory, there stands on the heathland south of Exning we now call Newmarket, six miles of earthwork fortifications known as the Devil's Dyke, dividing the July Course from the Rowley Mile.

Over a thousand years later, during the reign of Henry III, Sir Richard d'Argentine took for his bride the beautiful Cassandra d'l'Isle. Her marriage dowry included some land two miles southeast of Exning, and on this property her husband developed, literally, a New Market. The Market grew into a small town, the population swollen by the influx of people escaping the plague of 1227 and the citizens of Newmarket lived in prosperous and decent obscurity for the next four hundred years.

On 27th February, 1605, as one Guy Fawkes was digging tunnels and stacking gunpowder under the House of Lords, the worst royal rider ever to disgrace a saddle lurched across Newmarket Heath on his 'patent safety' as he followed a hare course near Fordham. This was His Majesty King James I of England and VI of Scotland, and that night he lodged at a hostelry called the Griffin, at Newmarket.

Realising that the Heath was prime sporting country, he promptly purchased the Griffin and moved his court to Newmarket, much to the annoyance of officers of his Government, obliged to make the weary journey from London on the State business cheerfully neglected by the sports-mad King.

The Griffin soon became too cramped for gay James's mixed retinue of effeminate favourites and rugged Scots courtiers. So, whilst dealing with the little local difficulty of the Gunpowder Plot, having Fawkes and his fellow conspirators hung, drawn and quartered, he commissioned the building of a palace at Newmarket.

Here, the King followed the hounds and went hawking while his courtiers raced horses, some of them a swift Spanish breed, descendants of equine survivors of the defeated Armada washed up on the Scottish shores of Galloway.

The first recorded match race at Newmarket

was on 8th March, 1622, but by 1625 King James was dying of the ague. His son, King Charles I, was a keen racing man and skilled horseman, and during his reign, sadly curtailed, the first grandstand was erected on Newmarket Heath.

Following Charles's execution in 1649, Cromwell's cheerless Puritan government broke up the royal studs at Hampton Court, Tutbury and Malmsbury. Although the intention was to dissipate the breed, in fact, the royal horses dispersed throughout the country attracted strong new bloodlines. So the Puritans inadvertently improved the stock from which the modern thoroughbred descends.

Restored to his rightful throne in 1660, King Charles II lost no time in restoring the fortunes of Newmarket as well. A new palace was built near the site of what is now the Rutland Arms Hotel (with the convenient addition of a secret passage to Nell Gwyn's house across the street). The Court moved to Newmarket in spring and autumn, and the Merry Monarch showed his skill as an amateur jockey in races across the Heath.

He recorded his first victory in the Town Plate on 14th October, 1671. He was successful at the Spring Meeting of 1675 and with the possible exception of Richard II in one of his rare light moments also at Newmarket, Charles is the only reigning sovereign to have ridden a winner.

As with his grandfather, affairs of State were neglected. One of his Ministers, Thomas Conway, found His Majesty was only able to conduct business when either in his bedroom, or (briefly) on waking from his post-prandial nap. There was no other time to spare from the pleasures of the

FATHER OF THE TURF, TREGONWELL FRAMPTON

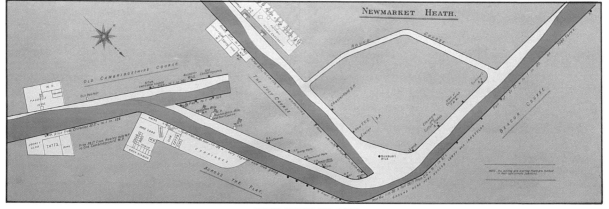

THE COURSE, 1903

bed, the table and the field.

The civic worthies of Oxford fared no better. Trying to present a petition concerning the Town-Clerkship of the city of dreaming spires, they had to waylay Charles at a race meeting on the Heath. The local racecourse roughs resented this interruption of the day's sport, and pelted the Mayor and Corporation with stones and mud. Things looked ugly until Nell Gwyn appeared on the scene, and hailed the King, 'Charles, I hope I shall have your company tonight, shall I not?'. All concerned dissolved in laughter, and the serious business of racing was resumed. The best-loved of all the royal mistresses, by both King and people, Nell Gwyn died in poverty at the age of 35. By two years, she outlived her regal lover, who said on his deathbed in 1685, 'Do not let poor Nelly starve'.

The King was dead, but under his patronage Newmarket had been established forever as the headquarters of racing. He also had a strong influence on breeding; part of the dowry of his luckless wife, the Portuguese Princess Catherine of Braganza, was a draft of Arab racehorses, swiftly absorbed in the re-stocking of the royal studs.

Charles's brother, James II, had too many political problems to care for the Sport of Kings, but his successor William III was a keen betting man, winning matches at Newmarket with horses rejoicing in the names of Cupid, Turk, Cricket and Stiff Dick.

His trainer, Tregonwell Frampton, held the appointment of 'Supervisor of the Race-Horses at Newmarket', a post he sustained through the reigns of the next three monarchs. He became known as the Father of the Turf, adjudicating in disputes and acting in effect as a one-man Jockey Club; he was racing's first administrator.

Some famous equine names started to grace the Heath. 'Flying' Childers beat Speedwell in a four-mile match at level weights on 26th April, 1721, and the next year he ran the six miles from Six Mile Bottom to the top of the July Course to

ECLIPSE

beat Chanter. Sired by the Darley Arabian, one of the three founding sires of modern racing, he was described as 'the fleetest horse that ever ran at Newmarket', a reputation based on only two races.

Next on the scene was the iron-grey Gimcrack, winner of twenty-five races before his final contest when he defeated eight rivals for a £50 prize at Newmarket in April 1771. This remarkable little horse also won a race against time in France in 1766, covering 22 miles and four furlongs in an hour.

In those days, horses rarely raced before they were five years old. A racing contemporary of Gimcrack was the superb Eclipse, foaled in 1764, the year of a total eclipse of the sun. He was unbeaten in 18 starts in 1769 and 1770, although seven were walk-overs. As a stallion, Eclipse's influence for speed transformed the breed, especially when combined with the sturdy stock of Herod; both horses were bred by the Duke of Cumberland.

Eclipse was owned for most of his career by Colonel Dennis O'Kelly, the Irishman of humble parentage, who attempted to work his way up the social ladder via billiard rooms, the Fleet Debtor's prison, and a purchased commission in the Middlesex Militia. The latter honour was originally due to the generosity of a helpful lady, Mrs Charlotte Hayes.

Immensely successful in his career on the Turf, O'Kelly was always denied the one thing he really craved: social recognition by the swells of the racing fraternity. Excluded from the merry-makers thronging the fashionable Assembly Rooms at York when Eclipse won in August 1770, O'Kelly was also refused admission to the Jockey Club, which precluded him from entering horses in many of the Newmarket stakes races. It is likely that the Colonel's only crime was to own the best horse of his generation, since the 'green ey'd monster' knows no class distinction. It must at least have been some satisfaction to him to hear the phrase coined, 'Eclipse! and nothing else', a wager which has gone down in Turf history as 'Eclipse first, the rest nowhere,' when the O'Kelly's beloved champion won his last competitive race at Headquarters. At least, that is how James Whyte described what is probably the most famous bet in racing history. Others would have it otherwise, and claim that O'Kelly, privy to gallops information, struck the wager after Eclipse had beaten Gower, Chance, Tryal and Plume in the first four-mile heat of the Noblemen and Gentlemen's Plate of 50 pounds 'for horses that never won 30 pounds (matches excepted)' at Epsom on Eclipse's first appearance on Wednesday, 3rd May, 1769.

The bet was that Eclipse would 'distance' i.e. win by at least 240 yards, in the second heat; this feat was easily achieved by Eclipse, but we have no record of the odds obtained by O'Kelly, who could have laid 4/1 with the leggers in the first heat.

Some reports suggest that O'Kelly invested his money on Eclipse's second appearance at Ascot three weeks later when he easily defeated his only opponent, Mr Fettyplace's Cream de Barbale, in the course of a couple of two-mile heats; but though the victory was easy, on neither occasion did Eclipse distance his rival.

Which brings us to Eclipse's second season in 1770. Now a six-year-old he defeated Bucephalus in a match at Newmarket, with his then owner, William Wildman (albeit with O'Kelly holding a half share), staking '600 guineas to 400 guineas, play or pay, on Eclipse'.

Not the level of stakes to appeal to O'Kelly, a man who bet in thousands, but typical of the provincial butcher Wildman; all of which lends credence to Whyte's theory that the historic wager was laid by O'Kelly at Newmarket in the same month, 19th April, when Eclipse beat Diana, Pensioner and Chigger in the first heat of a four-mile contest for the King's Plate of 100 guineas; in the second heat, Eclipse double distanced the field, O'Kelly having laid odds of ten to one 'and posted them'; the betting was to an 'immense amount' and called upon to declare, the then 'Captain' O'Kelly made his famous pronouncement, on the first occasion when Eclipse had run in his colours as sole owner.

O'Kelly took such exception to the gentlemen of the Jockey Club (or the 'black-legged fraternity' as he referred to them) for their snobbish behaviour, that he contracted his jockeys on the basis that they were free to take outside rides, if not required by O'Kelly, excepting any ride offered by Jockey Club members.

The history of the Jockey Club is an interesting one. In the mid-eighteenth century, anyone who had to do with horse racing was known as a jockey, or 'jockie' in the contemporary spelling, and the jockeys were in the habit of meeting in their clubs and coffee houses to settle bets and arrange further races.

Their favourite rendezvous was the Star and Garter in Pall Mall. In typically British fashion they did not publish a constitution or manifesto (much to the satisfaction of the historian Robert Black, writing in 1891 and deploring the French Société d'Encouragement's action in doing precisely that), but they formed a club in about 1750 with the good old British intention of protecting themselves from undesirable outsiders.

This latter class certainly included the professional riders we now know as jockeys. They were then simply servants or training grooms employed by the owners. Then, as now, servants were not elected to gentlemen's clubs, which is why there are no jockeys in the Jockey Club, much to the mystification of modern observers of the social scene.

It was clear that the Club would spend much of its collective time at Newmarket and in 1752 a lease was negotiated for a plot of land in Newmarket High Street and a Coffee Room was built, which almost certainly is the site of the Jockey Club Rooms today.

The lease was taken over by Captain Richard Vernon, also known as 'Jockey' Vernon or 'the oracle of Newmarket'. Vernon won the Club's first exclusive Plate in 1753 and also the inaugural Jockey Club Challenge Cup with Marquis in 1768.

By 1758 the Club was pontificating on such subjects as overweight and the rules for weighing out and in. It had clearly taken over the administration of racing which had been without proper guidance since the death of Tregonwell Frampton thirty years before. By 1831 the Club had bought the freehold of the Rooms and were already the owners or lease-holders of most of Newmarket Heath. They were in a position to extend their influence to control the whole sphere of British racing. Soon the words of the dreaded phrase 'warned off Newmarket Heath' were to ban the offender from taking part in racing anywhere in the British Isles, and nowadays this prohibition covers the civilised world.

The first real test of the Club's hegemony had

TOD SLOAN

been in 1791, when royal jockey, Sam Chifney Snr, was considered guilty of stopping the Prince of Wales's horse, Escape, in a blatant case of in-and-out running on successive days, contrived to suit the rider's own betting book. Interestingly, jockeys were allowed to bet at the time. Chifney did not back Escape in the first race when he started favourite, but had twenty guineas on when the horse was at 5/1 and won easily the next day.

It was a situation familiar today insofar as Chifney had long been suspected of chicanery, but the Jockey Club Stewards, headed by Sir Charles Bunbury, had no proof. Softly, softly, catchee monkey; even this case was hard to prove as the two races were over varying distances, but Bunbury's subtle mind was equal to the occasion.

THE TWO THOUSAND GUINEAS – GOING DOWN TO THE POST, 1874

The excuses trembling on Chifney's lips were ignored and Bunbury went straight to the jockey's employer, informing the Prince that 'if Chifney were suffered to ride the Prince's horses, no gentleman would start against him'.

This was as close to being warned off as royalty could be, and the future King George IV left Newmarket, never to return. The authority of the Jockey Club was established forever in a manner which the governing bodies of some other sports might well envy today.

By the late eighteenth century, three of the five classic races had been established: the St Leger, the Oaks and the Derby. Astonishingly, none was run at Headquarters but Newmarket remedied the omission in 1809 when Wizard, ridden by Bill Clift, won the inaugural Two Thousand Guineas over the Rowley Mile. The first One Thousand was run in 1814 and Charlotte was the winner, completing a unique double for jockey Bill Clift and owner Christopher Wilson.

Both Clift and Wilson came from Yorkshire, although from opposite ends of the social scale. Clift started life as a shepherd boy on the estate of the Marquis of Rockingham and attracted the attention of his influential employer when riding ponies in races arranged to amuse the Marquis's guests at Wentworth Woodhouse. A hard jockey, Clift was relentless with the whip, but he won thirteen classics, including five Derbies.

'Kit' Wilson is described by James Rice in his *History of the British Turf*, as an 'English gentleman of the old school, keeping up the old customs and liberally dispensing hospitality at his residence at Oxton House, near Tadcaster'. Wilson was certainly a great racing buff, and rarely missed a meeting at Epsom, Ascot, Newmarket, York or Doncaster. Apart from his success in the Two Guineas races, he also won the Derby and St Leger of 1800 with Champion.

As with the senior classics, the Guineas were for three-year-olds only. The early eighteenth-century custom of rarely racing horses before they were five had slowly been eroded. Four-year-old racing had been recorded as early as 1727 and Newmarket staged its first four-year-old event in 1744, followed by three-year-old races in 1756. Sir Charles Bunbury did much to pioneer the concept of races for younger horses over comparatively short distances to improve the speed of the breed, and two-year-old racing was to follow. In 1786 the Jockey Club instituted the oldest regularly run race for juveniles, the July Stakes.

In the mid-nineteenth century, eighteen courses were listed at Newmarket, including races run on what we now know as the July Course, and a yearling course of two furlongs and 147 yards. Happily, yearling racing did not catch on, and was officially banned by the Jockey Club in 1859.

James Whyte, in his 1840 *History of the Turf*, finds Newmarket 'the classic ground' of racing and goes on to assert that, 'it is here only that this delightful sport may be said to exist in perfection. No crowd, no booths impede the view; none of those discordant sounds which make a perfect Babel of other racecourses distract the attention. The number of spectators seldom exceeds five hundred, and they are mostly of the highest classes, the majority on horseback, with perhaps a few close carriages and barouches for invalids and ladies.'

Racegoers surveying the crowd's behaviour at Newmarket in 1988, when a man was killed in an ugly brawl adjacent to the July Course, might yearn for the example of our ancestors; but Victorian Newmarket was already experiencing problems of a different kind.

The concern was not the courses but the training grounds. The severe methods employed to prepare horses at the time resulted in many breakdowns. Owners tended to blame the gallops baked in the summer sun. On top of this, many rich racing men had withdrawn to their country estates following the Napoleonic Wars, spending less time in London. This minor social revolution in the habits of the landed gentry did Newmarket no good at all; handy for London, it was all but inaccessible from the shires.

Even that pillar of the Jockey Club, Lord George Bentinck did not support the town in its hour of need and had his horses trained in the 1840s at Goodwood. The nouveau riche merchants who were slowly to replace the aristocrats as racehorse owners in the aftermath of the Industrial Revolution, also found it more congenial to keep their horses in Epsom or Lambourn, far from the winter chills of the Heath.

Between 1788 and 1832, forty-one Derby winners were trained at Newmarket; in the following twenty-nine years, Headquarters provided only three winners of the premier classic. Two unrelated factors combined to revive the fortunes of Britain's finest home of the thoroughbred.

Firstly, the political unrest of Europe in 1848 had a devastating effect on the international horse trade, which had been of much benefit to Scottish trainers. A simultaneous decline in the fortunes of racing in Scotland eventually brought men such as Matt Dawson, his brothers Joe and John, and Jimmy Ryan, to open public stables in Newmarket where accommodation was cheap and plentiful.

The second factor was the developing interest

in racing shown by the Prince of Wales, probably the nearest thing to a reincarnation of Charles II that Newmarket could wish for. Unfettered by the cares of State, the Prince's first trainer, in 1886, was John Porter at Kingsclere in Berkshire. There was a clash of temperament between the fun-loving owner and his racing manager, Lord Marcus Beresford, also a man of humour, and the serious-minded trainer. The royal string was switched into the care of Richard Marsh at Newmarket at the end of the 1892 season, although the Prince and Porter remained on good terms.

By 1895, Mrs Edward Langtry, 'The Jersey Lily' and perhaps the Nell Gwyn of her time, was to be found at her racing stable, Ethelreda House, on the Exning Road. The name of the premises is a little ironic, as Ethelreda contracted two political and unconsummated marriages, founded a religious house at Ely, and was canonised.

The urbane Richard Marsh trained Persimmon to win the Derby and the Oaks in 1896, and Diamond Jubilee to win the Triple Crown in 1900. In 1909, Minoru won the Two Thousand Guineas and the Derby for the now King Edward VII.

It was the twentieth century and the glory days were back. There was no need for the Jockey Club to reduce one-third of the events at the second July Meeting to sellers in order to scrape up some revenue, as they had found necessary in 1890. Rather, it was a time to reflect on the great personalities of Newmarket. There was, of course, Fred Archer. Another Fred, Fred Webb, who was Lily Langtry's trainer and formerly a fellow apprentice with Archer, described his famous contemporary with a remark that could also apply

ROYAL TRAINER RICHARD MARSH

to another champion, recently retired: 'It's not the wasting that makes Archer so thin and worn. He wears that worried look because he can't ride two winners in one race.' The portly Dowager Duchess of Montrose, known as 'Old Six Mile Bottom' was supposedly in love with Archer; the romance foundered when the jockey discovered that the marriage would not make him a Duke.

JOE CHILDS, RIGHT, AND BROTHER CHARLES

There was Sir George Chetwynd, who resigned from the Jockey Club in disgrace after receiving an award of a farthing damages in a lawsuit following allegations that he had rigged races in collusion with his jockey, Charles Wood. George 'Abington' Baird, millionaire, amateur rider and lover of Lily Langtry was another. Warned off for foul riding at Birmingham, Baird sought his revenge on the Jockey Club by threatening to buy the lease of the Limekilns, one of the few gallops not owned by the Club. Baird was reinstated and the Jockey Club secured the Limekilns. Quite how this came about is uncertain. The Club had been happy to see the back of Baird, whose conduct suggested that he was every other inch a gentleman, and his excuse for attempting to put the Earl of Harrington over the rails at Birmingham, 'Beg pardon, I thought you were a bloody farmer', was unlikely to have cut much ice at the Club Rooms. Doubtless, a little Wilsonian pragmatism was employed by the Stewards.

By contrast, the Hon. George Lambton, brother of Lord Durham, who had exposed Sir George Chetwynd in a speech to the Gimcrack Club, was a resolutely honest master-trainer whose fifty-three-year career bridged the centuries. It was Lambton who uncovered the doping of horses by American trainers based in Newmarket at the turn of the century, which led to the Jockey Club issuing the first anti-doping rules in 1903. It was Lambton again who brought success in Britain to the first of the Eastern racing potentates when he founded the Aga Khan's breeding and racing empire in the early twenties.

'The lark's on the wing;

The snail's on the thorn:
God's in his heaven –
All's right with the world!'

So far as I know, the poet Robert Browning was not a racing man, but if he had been, those lines could well have described Newmarket's gentle July Course. A brother under the skin to the Rowley, the Bunbury Mile has a different personality. The Rowley is thrusting and purposeful, like those lantern-jawed gentlemen who leap over battlements to give ladies boxes of chocolates, while the Bunbury is easy-going, casual and would simply put the chocolates in the post. Spared the fulsome media coverage of Ascot and Goodwood, the Newmarket July Meeting is a genuinely relaxed treat for the racing connoisseur.

Amongst the beech trees, near the thatched roofed weighing room, the horses amble through the spinney of the pre-parade ring and the punters sip cool drinks at the outdoor bars and gossip as they make their selections. And yet, the most important role which the July Course had to play in the history of Newmarket came during the years when such silken dalliance had been replaced by the dogs of war in the two global conflicts of the twentieth century.

The shots from a Sarajevo street corner that killed Archduke Ferdinand of Austria in 1914 plunged Europe into a deepening battle and by May 1915 the Senior Steward of the Jockey Club was asked by the Government to suspend all race meetings for the duration of the war, except at Newmarket. In mid-June the first 'New Derby' was run over the July Course before a crowd more

CHARLIE ELLIOT, CHAMPION JOCKEY, 1924

concerned with events at Gallipoli and on the Western Front.

The winner was Pommern, trained by Charles Peck at Newmarket and ridden by Steve Donoghue, the first of six Derby victories for the newly crowned champion jockey. Pommern had won the Guineas and went on to take the September Stakes, regarded as the St Leger in 1915, and thus became the first war-time Triple Crown winner.

The following year, Fifinella won both the Derby and the Oaks over the July Course, in a welter of confusion over riding arrangements. The filly was trained privately at Newmarket by Dick Dawson and owned by the newspaper magnate, Edward Hulton. Hulton engaged Joe Childs to ride Fifinella in the One Thousand Guineas, although Donoghue had guided her to both her victories as a two-year-old.

Childs had to take leave from service with the 4th Hussars before he could accept the mount; he was a first-class jockey, but not well-tempered. Fifinella was wilful at the start of the Guineas and Childs clouted her with his whip; the filly sulked and would finish only second for her bullying rider.

Following this debacle, trainer Dick Dawson determined to engage Donoghue to ride Fifinella in the Derby and the Oaks, and Donoghue, who was a fine rider of temperamental fillies, declared himself available. On the morning of Derby Day, confusion reigned as Dawson's head lad handed the Hulton blue and orange silks to Donoghue, only for Childs to insist that the mount was his.

Finally, Childs took the ride and won on Fifinella by a neck, accusing Donoghue of foul riding on Steve's eventual mount, Flaming Fire. Donoghue was back in command in 1917 when Gay Crusader won the Derby for Mr Alfred Cox, the last owner of a classic winner to use the Victorian convention of a 'nom-de-course', being described on the racecard as 'Mr Fairie'. A lucky gambler, Cox's fortune stemmed from a seemingly worthless share in a run-down sheep farm won in a ship-board poker game en route for the antipodes. The farm turned out to be on the site of the Broken Hill silver mine.

Returning to England with rather more than the £100 he had set out with, Cox took up racing, Havana cigars and old brandy and Gay Crusader won a wartime Triple Crown for this man of good taste.

In 1918, fortune again smiled on 'Fairie' Cox and the irrepressible Donoghue when My Dear was awarded the Oaks in controversial circumstances following the disqualification of the first past the post, Stony Ford. Steve's old rival, Joe Childs, was also in form, winning the Derby on Lady James Douglas's Gainsborough, who galloped into the record books as the first Derby winner owned by a woman. Lady James was a member of the Anglo-French Hennessy family – doubtless 'Fairie' Cox enjoyed her homemade tipple – and Gainsborough was yet another Triple Crown winner, underlining the lack of competitive racing during the severe curtailment of the war years. This is well emphasised by Donoghue's jockeys' championship of 1916 with only forty-three winners, Childs finishing second with forty.

The 'War to End All Wars' finished in November 1918, and peace reigned for twenty-one

TRAINER FRED DARLING AT WORK, 1931

years; but by September 1939, the world was again on the verge of Armageddon. This time, the Rowley Course was requisitioned as an airfield and RAF Squadrons 138 and 161 flew Special Operations Executive agents into enemy occupied territory.

The July Course was now to stage twenty-seven classic races in six years and during the 'phoney' war the super-horse Djebel came from France to win the 1940 Two Thousand Guineas, ridden by Charlie Elliott. Djebel's remarkable record included fifteen wins from twenty-two starts, and he never finished out of the first three.

Hitler made sure that Djebel did not return to contest the Derby, and in the champion's absence, the winner was Pont L'Eveque, ridden by Sam Wragg, the middle brother of the three famous Wraggs, Harry, Sam and Arthur. Pont L'Eveque was the eleventh of trainer Fred Darling's nineteen classic winners, and should have been ridden by stable jockey Gordon Richards. But the man who was to become known as 'the shortest knight' preferred Tant Mieux, third in the Guineas behind Djebel.

The 1940 Oaks went to Godiva, ridden by seventeen-year-old apprentice Doug Marks, who'd won the One Thousand Guineas on the same filly, trained by William R. Jarvis at Newmarket. The Guineas win was easy, a five-length victory. The Oaks was another matter, as defeat stared Marks in the face when the 7/4 favourite lost many lengths at the start and was tailed off after four furlongs.

Doug Marks, the possessor of one of racing's

most original and civilised minds, was also a most sympathetic rider; Joe Childs could have taken lessons. As it was, Godiva scooted past the field three furlongs out to win by three lengths with Marks calling 'Come on!' to Gordon Richards and Tommy Weston on the runners-up.

By 1941, Gordon Richards' Derby jinx was becoming chronic. Tant Mieux wasn't the first wrong choice he had made, and in 1941 a broken leg forced him out for most of the season. This time it was the Fred Darling-trained Owen Tudor who won the Derby in the hands of Billy Nevett, the top northern jockey, who stood in for the hapless Richards.

Not everyone was happy as thousands flocked to the July Course to snatch a little colour from the dull grey of war. A cinema newsreel reporter was very pious; choking over his Woolton pie, he declared:

'We agree with the authorities that workers should have occasional relaxation, but we find it difficult to believe that there are tens of thousands of war workers who can be spared in mid-week or that the use of petrol to bring thousands of cars to Newmarket for the substitute Derby is helping the war effort. Our already heavily taxed railways have to run the trains in several sections and somehow these sort of things don't seem right in war-time; what do you think?'

The reporter then grudgingly described the race, concluding, 'Well, that takes care of another Derby; now let's win the big event'.

That season Commotion won the Oaks to continue the seemingly endless Fred Darling success story, with Harry Wragg doing duty for

OWEN TUDOR, RIDDEN BY TOP NORTHERN
JOCKEY BILLY NEVETT, SECOND RIGHT, WON
THE DERBY AT NEWMARKET , 1941

AERIAL VIEW, 1925

Richards on the way to the Head Waiter's only jockeys' championship. But the Richards luck was about to turn. The Derby was to prove elusive for eleven more years, but compensation was at hand.

Fred Darling had charge of a fine filly in Sun Chariot and also the superbly built colt Big Game. Both were leased from the National Stud, then based in Ireland, by King George VI. As always, royal patronage of racing caught the public imagination, and notwithstanding grumpy newsreel reporters, came as a tonic to a war-jaded Britain. Although wickedly temperamental, Sun Chariot proved to be a real champion.

Ridden by Harry Wragg in all her two-year-old starts, she went into winter quarters unbeaten as the first filly to win the Middle Park for twenty years. At three, Sun Chariot's temper was worsening and she was beaten at Salisbury when virtually refusing to race. However, she won the One Thousand Guineas easily enough by four lengths, but in the Oaks it looked like the Godiva saga all over again.

Sun Chariot was 4/1 on favourite. Diving left at the start and seemingly intent on racing on the Rowley Mile, she gave the field a furlong start before Richards could get her on an even keel.

SUN CHARIOT WON THE OAKS FOR KING
GEORGE VI, 1942

Catching up the stragglers with half a mile still to race, she made smooth progress to ruin the afternoon for Eph Smith and Tommy Carey as they watched the royal colours sail past to win by a length from Smith on Afterthought with Carey's mount Feberion third.

Sun Chariot went on to an easy victory over Watling Street in the St Leger, also on the July Course, and on her day she must have been one of the finest fillies ever to race.

Meanwhile, Big Game had won the Two Thousand Guineas by four lengths from Watling Street, but the day after Sun Chariot's Oaks, Watling Street emphatically reversed the form to run out an easy winner of the Derby with Big Game only sixth. Although he was sired by the Triple Crown winner, Bahram, Big Game did not truly stay a mile and a half, and reverting to ten furlongs he won the Champion Stakes from the long-suffering Afterthought.

The July Course had seen four classic victories in one season carrying the colours of King George VI, a feat unequalled by any monarch in racing history.

In 1943, there was another victory for a woman in the Derby when Miss Dorothy Paget's Straight Deal won by a head to emulate Gainsborough in 1918 and Mrs George Miller's Mid-Day Sun in 1937. But that classic year on the July Course really belonged to Lord Derby's Herringbone, winning two of the best races seen during the war.

Both were a tribute to the consummate jockey-ship of Harry Wragg. In the One Thousand Guineas, Herringbone won by a neck from Lord

JOCKEYS' ROOM, NEWMARKET, 1964

Rosebery's Ribbon, ridden by Eph Smith. She was only fourth in the Oaks behind Ribbon and the winner, Why Hurry, but in the St Leger she got up to win by a short head verdict over her old rival, Ribbon. In those pre-photograph finish days, it was a disputed decision, and many thought that poor Ribbon, now stuck with the unhappy reputation of being second in three classics, had got up.

1944 was the year of D-Day and the end of hostilities in Europe seemed in sight. Ocean Swell gave Billy Nevett another good chance ride in the Derby at 28/1, stable jockey Eph Smith having begged off to partner the unplaced favourite, Growing Confidence.

Berlin lay in ruins as the crowds flocked to Newmarket for the last of the war-time Derbies in 1945. Dante was favourite at 100/30. Beaten by a neck by Court Martial in the Guineas when blind in one eye, Dante won the Derby easily by two lengths, cheered home by the author, and a few others.

Trained at Middleham by Matt Peacock, Dante was the first northern-trained Derby winner since Pretender in 1869; and no northern contender has won since. Once again, Billy Nevett was the successful jockey, thus achieving the unique distinction of riding three wartime Derby winners.

So, peace returned to the July Course. The classics returned to the Rowley Mile and their other rightful homes at Epsom and Doncaster via the 1945 St Leger run at York. The beech trees sighed gently in the summer breeze, and a latter-day Browning may have mused over his champagne and reflected that the traditions handed down from the days of George Lambton through

TRAINER FRED DARLING

the eras of Boyd-Rochfort, Day, Butters and Murless to the custodians of today, such as Cecil, Stoute, Prescott, Brittain and Cumani, would have pleased Charles II. The King's nickname, 'Old Rowley', was derived from his favourite hack, afterwards a prepotent sire, the affectionate appellation reflecting the King's own prolific powers. For centuries it has also been the name of the principal course on the toughest, the finest and the fairest test of the thoroughbred anywhere in the world – Newmarket Heath. ∎

LORD DERBY'S GARDEN PATH, RIDDEN BY
HARRY WRAGG, WINNING THE TWO THOUSAND
GUINEAS, 1944

NOTTINGHAM

THREE HUNDRED years ago, in 1689, Nottingham Corporation resolved to subscribe towards a piece of plate to be run for at the racetrack on Basford Lings. The ultimate accolade of the period, a King's Plate, was first contested in 1727 and the course was reckoned to be 'a place of amusement in the racing line, (and) there are but few which are considered in any light in competition with it'.

Certainly, it was considered worth raising a subscription for the building of a grandstand designed by the leading racing architect, John Carr, following a grant of a lease on the land, originally part of Sherwood Forest, to a syndicate of local sportsmen, headed by Lord Edward Bentinck.

In 1797, part of the terrain was enclosed, and a Windsor-style figure-of-eight course was tried out with little success. A mile and a quarter circuit was then laid down and racing continued without interruption until 1831 when the meeting was abandoned as Nottingham Castle was set ablaze and there were riots prior to the Reform Act.

By 1839, Whyte was able to recommend the races, which took place about the middle of October and lasted for three days, on a course which was 'situated to the north-east of the town and is one of the finest and most ancient in the kingdom'. In 1846, when the track reverted to Corporation control, Nottingham was at the height of its nineteenth-century fame, and another meeting was established in the early fifties.

This was the apogee; Nottingham races fell into decline in the face of the same middle-class nonconformist conscience which will probably never allow Sunday racing in Britain, and racing was abandoned in 1890.

Two years later, the Colwick Racing and Sporting Company had the enterprise to set up a new course on the present site by the River Trent at Colwick Park. Things were not easy; in common with Leicester and Birmingham, Nottingham was unable to secure social patronage, which was essential to any sporting undertaking at the time.

Nonetheless, Nottingham was able to capitalise on its geographical convenience for northern and southern training centres alike and continued to provide bread-and-butter sport until 1965, when the Corporation purchased the 293-acre park for £5,000,000. For a while, the future of the course hung in the balance, until the Levy Board, under the chairmanship of Lord Wigg, came to the rescue and financed much-needed improvements.

Racing secure, commercial sponsorship was found to increase the value and the quality of the races, and neither the triple classic winner Oh So Sharp nor Derby victor Slip Anchor was ashamed to make a winning debut at Nottingham.

In 1986, vandals broke into the grandstand and set fire to the roof; extensive rebuilding was required, and as I write further refurbishment is in hand to ensure comfortable racing in the future.

But perhaps Nottingham will be best remembered by the present generation of racegoers as the scene of Lester Piggott's final bow.

Although the fates have not been kind to Piggott since, no-one who was present when he rode Full Choke to win the Willington Handicap Stakes on 29th October, 1985, will ever forget the emotion which the 'Longfellow' inspired. ■

LESTER PIGGOTT'S FINAL BOW, 1985

WARWICK

A PRAESIDIUM of the Romans, a fortress founded by Queen Ethelreda in 915, later built into a Norman castle by Geoffrey de Clinton; sometime home of Henry I; used as a military garrison by Henry III during a minor difficulty with the Barons, and headquarters of Warwick the Kingmaker during the seemingly interminable Wars of the Roses, Warwick is a place steeped in the history of England.

Even today, a true masochist can visit the torture chambers at the Castle in the morning and attempt to find a winning favourite at a Bank Holiday meeting in the afternoon.

Races were probably held as early as 1714, and certainly in 1728, when a warm August day attracted, amongst others, Mrs Archer and Mrs Bromley of Cambridgeshire 'loaded with jewels'; although it seems there were not many beauties present, some 'very agreeable young women' made the day for the young blades on Lammas Field.

By 1754, a two-day meeting was firmly established in August, with a hunters' race on the first day, and a £50 condition event on the second. A similar card was still on offer in 1783, when it was announced that the runners for both plates were to be 'shewn and entered' at the Cross-Keys Inn in Castle Street on Friday 22nd August between four o'clock and seven in the evening.

Early in the next century, a 'commodious' grandstand was erected by private subscription and in 1815 the two-mile circuit was considered by an observer to be 'one of the best in the kingdom'. By 1825, an estimated 50,000 spectators assembled for the second day, and Warwick had reached the height of nineteenth-century popularity when a

steeplechase course was built and the 1848 Grand National winner Chandler made his famous thirty-nine foot leap to clear a brook and four fallen horses in the 1847 Leamington Hunt Club Steeplechase.

At this time, there were two meetings annually: a one-day event in March featuring a £25 Plate donated by the ladies of Leamington, and the old August fixture spread over three days in September, including a Queen's Plate and the £100 Warwick Cup. The theatre was open during race week, starring mummers from the Cheltenham company, fairly fresh from their exertions in entertaining the racegoers at the July meeting over the Improved Old Course on Cleeve Hill; Cheltenham was then a flat race fixture, although steeplechasing had taken place intermittently since 1834.

Sad to relate, Warwick soon entered the doldrums, and the meeting was becalmed in the backwaters of the sport until a Warwick Races Club Syndicate formed in 1886 restored some semblance of the former glory. The Syndicate survived for sixty years until the Corporation purchased the course, in turn selling out to the Levy Board subsidiary, Racecourse Holdings Trust, in 1967.

Nowadays, Warwick would never be described as fashionable; rather, in the words of Howard Wright in the 1986 edition of *The Encyclopedia of Flat Racing*, the course 'provides opportunities for moderate horses to make some contribution towards their keep'.

To end with a story, probably apocryphal; many years ago, in the days of the old barrier start, Gordon Richards got a flier in the first. That doyen of the Turf, Charlie Smirke, thought the starter

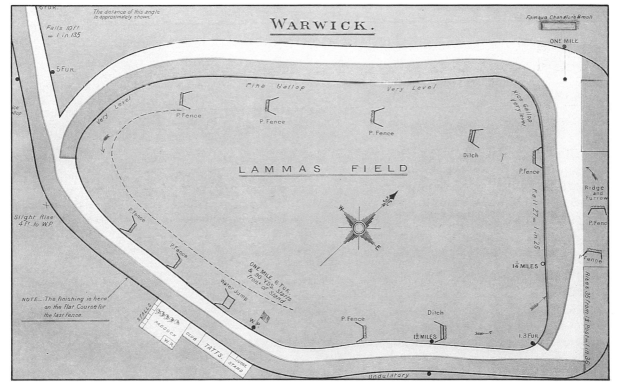

THE COURSE, 1903

was being unduly indulgent to Gordon, and as the field moved in for the second race, the following dialogue ensued.

Smirke: (to Starter) 'You can't possibly let them go, Gordon isn't ready.'

Starter: 'Don't be impertinent, Smirke.'

Smirke: 'I beg your pardon, sir, *Mr Richards* isn't ready.' ■

WOLVERHAMPTON

RACING STARTED at Wolverhampton in 1825 and in the 1840s the town of 20,000 inhabitants could offer the racegoer entertainment at the theatre and evening functions at the assembly rooms as diversions from the three-day August meeting held in parkland owned by the Marquis of Cleveland, formerly Lord Darlington.

The card was modest, the principal race on the first day being the Wolverhampton Stakes, a handicap sweepstakes of twenty-five sovereigns, with a hundred sovereigns added. The second day sported a rather ambitiously entitled St Leger Stakes over a mile and three quarters, for three-year-old colts and fillies, with fifty sovereigns added, together with the hundred sovereign Cleveland Cup, presumably in honour of the Dukedom bestowed on the Marquis in 1833.

The final day included a thirty sovereign sweepstakes for two-year-olds. This was the Holyoake Stakes, a handicap of twenty sovereigns each, the second to save his stake and the winner to pay ten sovereigns 'towards the expenses of the course'. The day wound up with the Himley Park Stakes, a consolation event with twenty-five sovereigns added 'for beaten horses'.

The racing was popular and well attended. It came as a grave disappointment to local sportsmen when the course was forced to close in 1878 after the Cleveland family sold the property to the Corporation for use as a public park.

The Jockey Club were petitioned, and in 1887 the Dunstall Park Club Company Limited was formed to buy a one hundred and thirty acre site a dual purpose course was laid out, permanent buildings erected and by the turn of the century,

ENCLOSURE, 1974

F.H. Bayles was enthusing, 'What a clever idea was embraced when Dunstall Park was secured for the purposes of racing, and a very well-managed meeting it is . . . arrangements to meet every requirement are made on the ground, while the races are wonderfully well attended socially, which speaks volumes for the manner in which it is possible to govern a racing crowd, even in this densely populated district of industry.'

So Wolverhampton proceeded for the next sixty years, until a period of decline put the course in danger of closure from lack of support. However, greatly improved amenities saved the day, and today the course does its best to make life easy for the racegoer, with a parade ring in front of the stands accessible to all enclosures, saddling boxes in view of any patron, and the author can personally vouch for the comfort and warmth of the glass-fronted bar with a fine vantage point from which to follow the running. ∎

Wolverhampton

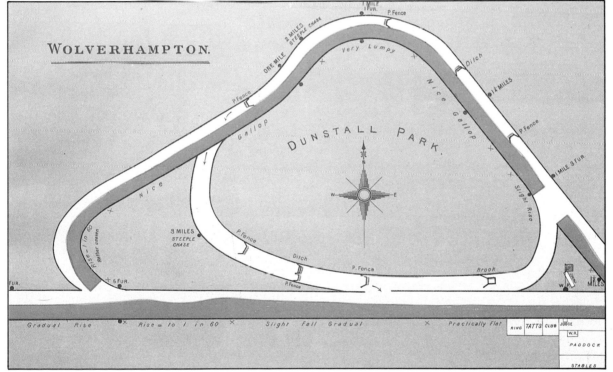

THE COURSE, 1903

139

YARMOUTH

THE GEOGRAPHER, geologist and Turf pundit, F.H. Bayles, did not have a lot of time for Yarmouth. In 1903, he considered the old track on the South Denes described by Tennyson as 'the long, low lines of tussocked dunes' to be crude in layout with abominable amenities and a racing surface beyond redemption.

Bayles reckoned that without the support of 'the Newmarket people regarding the dates in the light of a holiday . . . for 85 per cent of the horses that run at the meeting come from the headquarters of the turf, although they are at best but poor representatives of the Newmarket stables', Yarmouth had no right to exist.

He was once more, as his other work shows, ahead of his time. Within sixteen years, racing was transferred to a new course on the North Denes, where it was possible to cultivate proper turf on a terrain relatively free of the 'blown sand and marine shingle' which had so literally got up Bayles's nose.

To be fair, the old South Denes course was never intended to be an Ascot of East Anglia. Founded in 1715 by a syndicate of publicans doubtless as interested in providing refreshment as they were in equine sports, the attractions included donkey races and the pursuit of a pig with a soapy tail, and the events were all part of the celebrations of Yarmouth's September Fair.

By 1810, the races were advertised in the *Racing Calendar* and a formal two-day meeting scheduled for 20th September, entries to Mr John Buck, Clerk of the Course, who was to be found, naturally enough, at the Three Wrestlers Inn.

The meeting soon became popular among all classes, with the gentry arriving by carriage as other racegoers steamed up the River Yare to the landing stages where local boatmen plied a profitable ferry trade. The card, although modest, provided a Gold Cup Stakes on the first day, with twenty sovereigns added, together with a £50 Plate; the second day offered another £50 Plate 'raised by subscription among the neighbouring gentry' and a Handicap Stakes of three sovereigns each, with £30 added 'by the tradesmen of the town'.

Such was the happy state of affairs in the mid nineteenth century before a few mean-minded local Justices of the Peace elected to prohibit all betting (either on or off the course) most of which was conducted in the pubs which served as the betting shops of the time.

Discreet pressure from the various vested interests persuaded the magistrates to rescind this ill-thought regulation. It would not, in any case, have deterred the ruffians who then as now threatened the genuine racegoers, and probably could not have been enforceable in any event.

In 1904, the lease on the South Denes and the grandstand expired and the Corporation appointed a committee of trustees to run the course, which was resited, complete with Old County Stand, at North Denes in 1919-20 as the coast was ameliorated for the benefit of the fishing trade.

Originally, the going in high summer was extremely dry and little better than on the scorned South Denes. In the twenties, when the father and son team of Felix and Jack Leach almost went through a two-day card, a disgruntled journalist wired to his paper: 'Yarmouth was all Leaches and dust'. An automatic watering system installed in 1960 has produced ground which is now generally good.

Jack Leach had an even better reason to remember Yarmouth. Arriving at the seaside course one day in the early years of the decade of cocktails and laughter, he encountered a desperate trainer; Harvey (Jack) Leader had engaged Michael Beary to ride two fancied animals but Beary had wired to cry off.

Luckily, Leach was free for the races concerned, and won on both horses. A delighted Leader decided to book Leach whenever he could in the future, which led to the jockey's association with the brilliant sprinter Diomedes, on whom he was victorious in sixteen races and dead-heated once, in the July Cup of 1926. Diomedes' other wins included the King's Stand Stakes, the Nunthorpe and the Portland Handicap.

Since 1965, Yarmouth has been under the control of the Borough Council, and, as in Bayles's day, very much Newmarket-by-the-Sea with many of the runners making the seventy-mile journey from Headquarters. Although occasionally a future equine star will make a debut on North Denes, it is generally the second-strings who make up the fields at this pleasant course which has now regained all of its Georgian and Victorian popularity with the crowds of East coast holidaymakers. Even so, it is easy to regret the passing of the soapy-tailed pig. ■

JACK LEACH

ASCOT

H ER MAJESTY QUEEN ANNE was married to Prince George of Denmark, described by some historians as an overweight virile glutton. The Queen endured eighteen pregnancies and bore six children, none of whom survived infancy, with one stillborn. It is perhaps not surprising that she was usually unwell and considered to be dull and uncharitable.

Into this unhappy regal existence, there shone two rays of light. Queen Anne was a niece of King Charles II and she inherited the Merry Monarch's love of the Turf. She was also fortunate in her choice of generals and politicians and when the war of the Spanish Succession was effectively ended by

QUEEN ANNE

the Duke of Marlborough's victories at Blenheim and Ramillies, peace came to Europe followed swiftly by the Act of Union with Scotland.

The Queen and her people were free to relax and enjoy the pleasures of sport, art, science and literature, all of which flourished during the renaissance of the new Great Britain. Commerce and agriculture also prospered, and it was against this background that Queen Anne made her now famous drive from Windsor Castle in the early summer of 1711.

Observing the natural advantages of Ascot Heath for her favourite sport, the Queen gave orders for a course to be prepared and announced her intention of donating a Queen's Plate. The tradition of Queen's (or King's) Plates, an early form of sponsorship in the guise of Royal Patronage had been instigated by Charles II, but before racing could take place the Duke of Somerset, Master of the Horse and acting as the first of Her Majesty's Representatives had to order an army of workmen into action.

No expense was spared. The principal contractor, William Lowen, charged £558. 19s. 5d for his work, no mean sum in 1711, while the carpenter William Erlybrow was paid £15. 2s. 8d for erecting the posts and rails.

Ben Culchett received £2. 15s. for painting, but a clerk, Mr John Grape made only a measly £1. 1s. 6d for drafting the conditions of the races.

However, the Queen's instructions were swiftly carried out and on 12th July 1711, gentlemen partaking of their favourite mid-morning beverage at the Star and Garter in Pall Mall and other London coffee houses were doubtless interested to learn from the *London Gazette* that 'Her Majesty's Plate of 100 guineas will be run for round the new heat on Ascot Common, near Windsor, on Tuesday, 7th August next by any horse, mare or gelding being no more than six years old in the grass before and must be certified under the hand of the breeder. Carrying 12st in three heats, to be entered the last day of July at Mr Hancocks at Fern Hill near the starting post'.

Another event, a 50 guinea plate, was announced for Monday, 6th August, but both races were postponed, probably because the course was not yet ready, but possibly because no-one had remembered to obtain the permission of the Lord of the Manor of Ascot.

So, four days late the Queen and what was described as 'a brilliant suite' drove from her castle to witness the fifty guinea plate. Royal Ascot had arrived and Her Majesty returned to the Heath in similar style on Monday, 13th August to see five runners go to post for the Queen's Plate.

Jonathan Swift, typical of some journalists even today, turned up late, complaining that 'everybody's coach had gone' and refusing to ride to the course.

Despite his known aversion to horseback, perhaps the Dean had simply enjoyed a good lunch; anyway, he had previously made contact with the Queen's physician Dr Arbuthnot and driven with him to inspect the course. En route, they overtook Miss Forester, a Maid of Honour to the Queen and the reigning beauty of the time. This lady had been a child bride, married at the age of ten to the son of Sir George Downing, the builder of Downing Street. Not surprisingly,

the union had been disastrous and was eventually dissolved.

Although the innocent party, Miss Forester remained something of a social outcast until the Queen appointed her a Maid of Honour. Normally meticulous in matters of dress herself, Queen Anne indulged her protégée's taste for eccentric high fashion and Miss Forester was to become a pioneer of Ascot style. She attended the first meeting in a long white riding coat with a full-flapped waistcoat and a small cocked hat, three-cornered and sporting gold lace trim, worn over a flowing white powdered periwig.

'Dressed like a man' as Swift dryly observed, doubtless sipping his bumper of claret; but in one season the spirit of Ascot, as the world was to come to know it, had been established. There was royalty, elegance and good living, high society and fashion with the society reporters of the day in attendance, ever eager to record the aristo's activities for the benefit of a drooling public.

The following year the meetings were held again in August with more in September. A 'brilliant company' attended the Queen in 1713, the year in which the Treaty of Utrecht put the seal on European peace and Anne's beloved Tory Party were firmly in power.

Perhaps now the lady who bequeathed us the traditions of Royal Ascot was truly happy; if so the happiness was to be short-lived. Queen Anne died on 1st August, 1714 and the meeting due to be run on the 13th was postponed for the period of mourning and ultimately abandoned.

Lean times were to follow. The Hanoverian George I was emphatically not a man of the Turf and cheerfully imprisoned his adulterous wife Sophia Dorothea for life, in the castle of Ahlden, in order to enjoy the company of two well-built mistresses known to the Londoners as the Elephant and Castle and The Maypole, more formally addressed as the Countess of Darlington and the Duchess of Kendal.

A few hunters' events were staged in 1720 and 1724 for members of The Royal Buckhounds, but racing languished without royal patronage and the succession of George II in 1727 did little to improve matters. The King was more interested in breeding than racing and although three-day fixtures had been established at Ascot by 1735, the course became reduced to the stature of a well-run but minor venue.

As such, Ascot fell victim to the Act of 1739 designed to suppress the host of minor meetings which had sprung up around the country and where cheating on the track and ruffianism off it were rife. Any prize of less than a £50 plate became illegal, and although Newmarket and York were exempt, Ascot was not, and without the King's Plates, could not afford the £50 limit.

Five years later, William Duke of Cumberland returned from his victory over the remnants of the Pretender's army at the Battle of Culloden. While Bonnie Prince Charlie consoled himself in exile with Drambuie and Flora MacDonald, Cumberland, who loved his racing, was appointed Ranger of Windsor Forest and set about restoring the fortunes of Ascot.

The Duke bred Eclipse, foaled in 1764 and destined never to be beaten. Sadly Cumberland died in 1765 before he could see Eclipse in action,

GEORGE III

but his main work was done. At no little expense to himself, he had set Ascot on the path to glory. His nephew, an equally enthusiastic racing buff, succeeded to the Dukedom and the post of Ranger and by 1768 King George III could drive to Ascot in state and find his subjects enjoying a five-day June meeting, with dancing nightly and a public breakfast at the Assembly Rooms, Sunninghill on the first day.

This was the year when Count Lauraguais's speedy grey Gimcrack won both heats of the Members' £50 Plate, and which saw the inauguration of the quaintly-named Yeoman Pricker's Plate.

The fun and games amongst the carriage set, then as now, reflected little of the activities on the

GEORGE IV

of the top jockeys of the day. Sam Chifney Jnr had the leg up on Zinganee, formerly owned by Chifney and now racing in the colours of Lord Chesterfield, while W.W. Wheatley steered the 1827 Derby winner Mameluke.

As the jockeys watched each other like hawks, with Wheatley taking a pull every time Chifney did the same, the contest became a hundred yard sprint as they passed the Betting Stand, with Zinganee and the crafty Chifney prevailing by a length.

It was Prinny's last Ascot. He had never satisfied his burning ambition to win a Gold Cup, although he could have had Zinganee for 2,500 guineas. Almost on his deathbed he ordered that future Cups should be confined to members of either the Jockey Club, Whites or Brooks. The effect of this uncharacteristic gesture on the entries can be imagined and in 1831 only two runners took part, albeit for a fine race, with Jem Robinson on Cetus beating Lord Exeter's Augustus by a head.

King William IV was not the keenest of racegoers, preferring the pleasures of sailing, and even his jockey was called Nelson, but he continued as patron of the Royal Meeting and presented a new trophy, the Eclipse Foot. This was a hoof of the great horse set in gold and was donated by the King when hosting the annual pre-Derby dinner at the Jockey Club on 16th May, 1832.

The prize money was 200 guineas, and the race was to be for horses owned by Club members only, on the principle that if it were to be a public event, the rare trophy might fall into disreputable hands. Since the Eclipse Foot was competed for on only four occasions and ended up as a snuff box in the

THE ROYAL PARTY IN THE QUEEN'S STAND, 1868

ça change; and when William Hubbert, Clerk of the Course, gave orders for an area of one hundred square yards to be enclosed in front of the Royal Stand, it was the early version of the exclusive Royal Enclosure.

In spite of the corruption rife in racing at the time, not known as the 'Filthy Forties' for nothing, Ascot continued to prosper as Britain's premier course. Admittedly, atrocious weather spoiled the fun of the bumper crowds assembled for the Great Exhibition year of 1851, and poor Nat Flatman, by now the first recorded champion jockey, was brought down on the Ascot Derby favourite Red Hand by a dog running across the course in 1852. Horse and rider were reunited safe and well; the fate of the dog is unrecorded.

By and large, it was still a time of expansion. The Queen's own enthusiasm remained unabated, and her excitement was so great when Monge won the New Stakes in 1854 that she broke a window in the Royal Stand. Doubtless the monarch had her money down.

By 1856, when Forbidden Fruit beat twenty-seven home in the Hunt Cup, the railway line had opened up, thus easing the traffic congestion on the coaching roads, and the Crimean War had ended with the capture of Sebastapol; the following year the Russian Ambassador was back with the royal party.

After the death of Prince Albert in 1861, Queen Victoria never went racing again. Her place was taken by the Prince of Wales, later Edward VII, appearing with his new bride, Princess Alexandra, in 1863 and again in 1864. There was no procession until 1866, however, the year when

Gladiateur, French-bred and dubbed the avenger of Waterloo after winning the Derby in 1865, won the Gold Cup by forty lengths.

A spring meeting was held as an experiment in 1867, but not with much success and it seemed that Ascot was to be centred on the four days of the Royal Meeting for many years to come.

By 1871 fashion was at its height again, led by the Princess of Wales in amber satin, black lace and bonnet to match. The gossip writers record the Duchesse d'Ossima in brown satin and yellow silk, and 'the beautiful Lady Mary Dawson attracted general admiration' in flounced pale primrose muslin; and this was to say nothing of the 'fascinating' Madame Becheve in dark blue velvet.

Great hospitality was dispensed by the officers of the Scots Fusiliers, the 7th Hussars and the 12th Lancers in their luxuriously furnished booths on the Heath, but significantly Isabella, toast of Longchamp and described as the favourite flower girl of the French Jockey Club, was refused admission to the Royal Enclosure. Perhaps this was because she was attired in chocolate and red, the colours to be carried by the French-trained Boiard, favourite and eventual winner of the 1874 Gold Cup.

No doubt Madamoiselle Isabella found a warmer welcome extended by the gallant gentlemen in their luxurious accommodation on the Heath; and so things continued on their merry way. Persimmon, Derby winner of 1896, won the Gold Cup for the Prince of Wales in his mother's Jubilee year of 1897, amidst appropriate jubilation.

More attention was now being paid to the

PERSIMMON AT STUD

662—THE ILLUSTRATED SPORTING
AND DRAMATIC NEWS—June 29, 1934

BROWN JACK
by
LIONEL EDWARDS

Pencil sketches from an artist's note-book

INSEPARABLE STABLE-COMPANIONS:
Brown Jack (on the right) with Mailed Fist

THE END OF THE DAY:
The evening nibble in the paddock

On right:
AFTERNOON
SIESTA: Brown
Jack "roosting"
on his manger

I FEEL that my illustrations of this animal require some comment. Brown Jack is far from a good-looking horse. I should guess that, under another name, his probable value in the open market, when his age and legs are taken into consideration, would be perhaps 60 guineas.

His history supports this view. Bred in Ireland, he was shown as a yearling in a local show. There were five entries, and he was placed fifth! Sent to Dublin, his owner did not at first get an offer for him. He started his racing life as a hurdler, and then showed such form that, after winning the Cheltenham Gold Cup, Donoghue was asked if he would care to ride him on the flat.

OFF TO MORNING EXERCISE: The string at Wroughton.
Brown Jack's trainer, Ivor Anthony, is on the right

BROWN JACK: FROM AN ARTIST'S NOTEBOOK

THE ILLUSTRATED SPORTING AND DRAMATIC NEWS—June 29, 1934—663

Some Everyday Incidents in the Stable Life of a Famous Thoroughbred

FINISHING UPHILL : A training gallop across the Bushes at Wroughton

*On left:
IN LIGHTER MOOD : Brown Jack steals his lad's cap*

THE FARRIER AT WROUGHTON : Brown Jack gets some new shoes

Having seen Brown Jack run, Donoghue at once closed with the offer. After losing his first flat race, the horse's subsequent career has been a series of triumphs.

But, if not much to look at, Brown Jack is a "character," and I think he wins by his brains. For example, he knows exactly if the ground will suit him or not. If it is too hard for his old legs he won't try—which is why he has lasted so long at such a strenuous life. A second reason is that, being intensely curious, he does not get bored with training, or, rather, he quickly shows when he is bored and would like a change of *terrain*. Hence the frequency with which he is trained on strange gallops.

Brown Jack is extraordinarily quiet and pleasant and likes to be made much of. He frequently has a children's "congregation" on Sundays—the children feed him in his box. His head is the head of a hunter, with a wise and kindly eye—hence my painting is a fairly good portrait of him, for, as his lad remarked : " You are the first painter not to try to make him look like a race 'oss, which is the last thing he looks like ! "

LIONEL EDWARDS

*On left :
RETURNING FROM EXERCISE : Brown Jack on his way back from the Downs*

IN HIS YOUNGER DAYS : Sir Harold Wernher's famous gelding training over hurdles at Wroughton, in Wiltshire

THE ROYAL PARADE, 1928

If Brown Jack was a hero, it would not be unfair to describe Pretty Polly and Quashed as heroines. Pretty Polly enjoyed a brilliant two-year-old career and was unbeaten in nine starts, twice defeating the future Derby winner St Amant. By the end of the season she was the idol of the racing public, and went on to win the 1,000 Guineas, the Oaks and the St Leger.

Among her victories as a four-year-old, she won the Jockey Club Cup rather unconvincingly from Bachelor's Button, who was something of an Ascot specialist. But if there was any sense of foreboding in the torrid air as the field paraded for the 1906 Gold Cup, it was lost on the sweltering crowd of admirers who had made Pretty Polly 11/4 on favourite.

Admittedly, she was reluctant to leave the paddock, possibly upset by the crowds. She was also suffering from a wart on her belly, and this time the connections of Bachelor's Button had decided to run a pacemaker, a useful horse called St Denis, who had been third in St Amant's Derby.

Pretty Polly ran her usual brave race, but it was not to be. The cheers as she struck the front in the hands of Bernard Dillon turned to shocked silence when Danny Maher produced Bachelor's Button for a perfectly timed run to wear down the First Lady of the Turf and win by a length.

Excuses were made, as they were made after Petite Etoile was beaten by Aggressor in the 'King George' nearly sixty years later. Many blamed Dillon as in the latter case they were to blame Piggott, but needless to say, the punters still loved the elegant Pretty Polly, who had run her last race.

Quashed had none of the precocious brilliance of Pretty Polly, and was allowed to start at 33/1 for the 1935 Oaks, which she won by a short head. Unthinkably by today's standards, she contested long-distance handicaps during the remainder of her three-year-old season, in addition to winning the Jockey Club Cup.

The spring of 1936 found this tough filly dead-heating with Jack Tar, who was receiving twenty-six pounds, for the Great Metropolitan Handicap at Epsom and beating Cecil by a neck in the Ormonde Stakes at Chester. By now Quashed, like Pretty Polly and Brown Jack, had caught the imagination of the public for her sheer bravery, and but for the awesome reputation of the 1935 American Triple Crown winner, Omaha, would have started a warm favourite for her next race, the Ascot Gold Cup.

As it was, Quashed was 3/1 second market choice to William Woodward's 11/8 favourite, now trained by Cecil Boyd-Rochfort, and winner of both his races in England. There were three French contenders in the field plus the Yorkshire Cup winner Valerious, and Robin Goodfellow, second in the 1935 Derby.

Both Quashed and Omaha were dropped out for the first half of the race, but Dick Perryman sent Quashed into the lead as they turned for home. From the bell Quashed raced on the rails with Omaha making steady ground. The American horse, ridden by Rufus Beasley, looked the winner with a furlong to go and hit the front a hundred yards from the post.

Quashed seemed beaten, but as usual would not give in. Beasley went for his whip, dropped it,

and at this crucial moment Omaha hung slightly left, away from Quashed. It was all that was needed; the mare passed the post a short head to the good.

It had been a desperate battle and Quashed had needed to call on every ounce of her remarkable courage, a fact which did not go unnoticed by her many supporters. When her number was hoisted into the frame, a hurricane of cheers reverberated across the Heath.

Since the war, Ascot has expanded from the four days of the Royal Meeting and now sports five fixtures and a total of thirteen days' racing a year. There is also a fine National Hunt course, albeit once described by a well-known owner and breeder as 'Blackpool with the tide out'.

The shadow of death fell across Ascot Heath in 1959, when Manny Mercer was thrown from Priddy Fair on the way to post for the Red Deer Stakes on 26th September, 1959. The jockey's head hit the concrete support of the rails, and the filly kicked Mercer in the face as she struggled to her feet. Mercer, the elder brother of Joe Mercer, had enjoyed a brilliant career in the saddle after winning the 1948 Lincolnshire Handicap on 100/1 chance Jockey Treble. He rode over a hundred winners in four seasons and took the 1953 One Thousand Guineas on Happy Laughter and the Two Thousand with Darius in 1954.

Aside from the Royal Meeting, Ascot's principal race is the King George VI and Queen Elizabeth Stakes run over a mile-and-a-half in late July. Originally founded as the King George VI and Queen Elizabeth Festival of Britain Stakes in 1951 as part of the festival designed to com-

QUASHED, ASCOT GOLD CUP WINNER, 1936

memorate the 1851 Great Exhibition and to stimulate Britain's post-war revival, and the brain-child of Sir John Crocker Bulteel, Ascot's finest administrator, the Roll of Honour includes no fewer than twelve Derby winners and such names as Dahlia, Ribot, Ballymoss and Aureole.

In prestige the 'King George' competes only with the Grand Prix de l'Arc de Triomphe as a test for three-year-olds and upwards and in 1975 produced one of the greatest races in English history when Grundy held on to win after a titanic struggle with Bustino from a field which included the 1973 and 1974 winner Dahlia, and 1974 Arc winner Star Appeal.

From the early sixties, Ascot racegoers have enjoyed the facilities of a superb cantilever stand, built following a re-alignment of the straight mile in 1952, and even if a wise man needs to take a hip flask on Gold Cup day when your chances at the bar are slightly worse than going through the card, who cares when you're present at the finest festival of racing in Europe – probably in the world. ■

THE TITANIC STRUGGLE BETWEEN GRUNDY
AND BUSTINO IN THE 'KING GEORGE', 1975

Dennis O'Kelly, who all went pot-hunting at the new meeting.

Only Bunbury was successful, with his mare Eliza taking the Gentlemen's Plate on the second day, starting 2/1 second favourite. O'Kelly's Adjutant let down the local punters at 7/4 on in the first day's sweepstake for older horses, whilst Richmond's unnamed chestnut colt was distanced in the second heat, and thus eliminated from the contest.

Backers did little better in the pony race, with the even money favourite, Mr Dymock's brown gelding, finishing only fourth.

'Twas ever thus, I dare say; but as the *Calendar* continued to advertise racing from such long lost venues as Grantham, Basingstoke, Oxford and Canterbury, to say nothing of horse medicines including purging balls at 2/- a parcel, Brightelmstone's fortunes were assured by no less a figure than the Prince of Wales, later Prince Regent and eventually King George IV.

Prinny's Pavilion at Brighton was not completed until 1787, but he and his bucks found enjoyment in the fine Sussex air at Brightelmstone Races a little earlier, in 1784. The bucks discovered much amusement in jumping their horses over the sheep hurdles on the Southdown hills, thus paving the way for Brighton's unlikely career as a National Hunt venue in the nineteenth century, since few courses could have been so unsuited by conformation to hurdle racing.

The Prince's name appears amongst the subscribers to races at Brightelmstone in 1785, in the Conflans Stakes of fifty guineas each, with the interesting condition that 'horses bred in France

THE BEST VIEW, BRIGHTON, 1968

and it is an interesting coincidence that the two premier races under both codes, the Derby and the Cheltenham Gold Cup, are both run in the vicinity of spa towns.

Epsom would have to wait half a century for its rebirth; since 1730 two annual race meetings had been established, courtesy of Lord Baltimore of Woodcote Park, whose successor was obliged to leave the country in 1769 after being acquitted of the rape of Sarah Woodcock, a milliner. Lord Baltimore then travelled Europe with eight women, two black eunuchs and, wisely, a physician. Not surprisingly, Baltimore died in Naples in 1771 leaving the Banstead Downs unencumbered for the continuance of some of the most boring racing then taking place in Britain.

It was the era of heats, usually over two or four miles, and it took all day to decide the outcome of one contest. The races were reasonably well endowed with £50 plates sponsored by local tradesmen who made a good income from booths and catering stalls, and the public turned up in reasonable numbers. So things might have continued but for a thread of events which had originated in a two-mile race for three-year-olds run on the Beacon Course at Newmarket in 1756.

The attraction of a pillar-to-post contest was obvious, but it was not until Col. Anthony St Leger had inaugurated the classic subsequently named after him in 1776 that such events became popular. 1776 was a difficult year for Britain; the American colonists had become tiresome, as colonists will, and one of three generals sent by the Prime Minister, Lord North, to restore order in the Home of the Brave and end the war was 'Gentleman Johnny' Burgoyne.

Burgoyne, in the cliché, was a man of many talents. Reputedly an illegitimate son of Lord Bingley, he was forced into exile in France after eloping with Lady Charlotte Stanley, daughter of the 11th Earl of Derby. Later reconciled with the Derby family, Burgoyne leased his mansion, The Oaks, which he had developed from an old alehouse, to Edward Stanley, later the 12th Earl of Derby.

'Gentleman Johnny' also excelled as a playwright, and wrote a masque called 'The Maid of The Oaks' which was staged by David Garrick in the grounds of the house as part of the celebrations at a fête-champêtre in honour of the engagement of the future Earl to Lady Elizabeth Hamilton in 1774. Garrick was to use 'The Maid of The Oaks', which has all the classic ingredients of eighteenth-century comedy, including rustics, irascible aristocrats and deliberate mistaken identity, as a Christmas entertainment for some years. But Burgoyne was to come to grief as the commander of the British troops who surrendered ignominiously at Saratoga in 1777, the victims of political bungling.

Returning home in misery and unfair disgrace, Burgoyne sought refuge with his nephew by marriage at The Oaks. During his absence in America, Lady Charlotte had died, and Edward Stanley had succeeded his grandfather and become the 12th Earl of Derby. Forced into idleness, Burgoyne advised Derby on the latter's bloodstock interests and persuaded him to emulate Burgoyne's old comrade-in-arms, Anthony St Leger, and found a race for three-year-olds. Confined to fillies and named after The Oaks, the inaugural

Epsom

event over one-and-a-half miles was won by Lord Derby's Bridget on 14th May, 1779.

Flushed with success, on the night of Bridget's victory, Derby gave a sumptuous dinner party at The Oaks. The guests included Charles James Fox, wit, philosopher, writer and leading Whig politician; Richard Brinsley Sheridan, parliamentarian, playwright and author of *The Rivals*, one of the finest plays in the English language; General Burgoyne, and Sir Charles Bunbury, Steward of the Jockey Club and House of Commons colleague of Fox in the campaign to abolish the slave trade.

As the gentlemen caroused into the night, they came upon the idea of another race, for three-year-old colts and fillies, to be run over the mile course which in those days started half a mile east of Tattenham Corner. Colts were to carry 8st and fillies 7st 11lb; all that was now required was a name for the race.

Naturally, it would honour one of the co-founders, but how to decide; dice were rolled, or cards were drawn, tossed coins being a matter of mythology. It could have been the Fox, the Sheridan, the Burgoyne or the Bunbury, but either by chance or gentlemanly design, the honours went to the host, and it was the Derby Stakes which Diomed won in the pink and white striped colours of Sir Charles Bunbury on Thursday, 4th May, 1780.

Derby and Bunbury: two classic cases of 'unlucky in love, lucky at cards'. The fire of love which had burned so brightly for Derby and Lady Elizabeth at Burgoyne's fête-champêtre only five years before turned to cold clinker when she absconded with the Duke of Dorset almost as Sam

Arnull steered Diomed to victory. Meanwhile Bunbury had endured the misfortune of marriage to Lady Sarah Lennox, daughter of the second Duke of Richmond. When this lady took up residence with Lord William Gordon, Bunbury was all for pistols at dawn until it was indicated to the cuckolded baronet that he would have to challenge most of London society to gain adequate satisfaction.

Both gentlemen were to return to the condition quaintly described by the historian John Orton as 'the joys of Hymen'. Bunbury had a happy if childless second marriage, and Derby gained consolation with the actress Elizabeth Farren, popularly known as Eliza. The Earl fell in love with her when she played the lead in a play by Burgoyne, *The Heiress*; later she starred in Sheridan's *The School for Scandal* as Lady Teazle, and the enamoured Earl named his 1787 Derby winner Sir Peter Teazle, sired by the Bunbury-bred stallion Highflyer, in her honour.

The cosy social cabal of Derby, Burgoyne, Sheridan, Bunbury & Co. went to some lengths to exclude the upstart Dennis O'Kelly, the former sedan-chairman and Irish expatriate inmate of the Fleet debtors' prison. He was, at the time, living in style at Clay Hill, Epsom, with his wife and benefactress Charlotte Hayes, London's leading brothel-keeper.

O'Kelly had bred some useful horses by Eclipse, the finest horse of the eighteenth century, and standing at stud at Clay Hill. He was to sire the winners of 862 races worth £158,047 in stakes, including three Derby victors bearing the scarlet jacket and black cap of O'Kelly who cheerfully

THE DERBY, 1791

promoted himself from Major to Colonel as a celebration of Young Eclipse's win in 1781.

The socially spurned O'Kelly would have given his left ear to win the inaugural Derby, and he nearly did. Although the distances are not recorded, the Irishman's Budroo finished second to Diomed for the prize of £1,065. 15s. The starting prices were returned as 6/4 Diomed, 4/1 Budroo, 7/1 Spitfire, who finished third, and 10/1 bar in a field of nine.

O'Kelly gained some compensation when his King Fergus, another of Eclipse's progeny, won the next race on the card in three four-mile heats, the Noblemen and Gentlemen's Purse. King Fergus won the first heat, was clearly given a breather in the second when finishing only sixth, but cantered up in the third to take the stakes from Mr Hull's chestnut horse Epsom.

Neither Dennis O'Kelly, nor anyone else on the Downs that sunny day in May realised that they were present at an event which was to be so important that men with riches beyond the dreams

MAMELUKE, DERBY WINNER, 1827

of avarice were prepared to cheat for victory. At least one woman was to use it as the instrument of ultimate sacrifice for her cause, and Eastern potentates of different generations would throw money at it like schoolboys hurling mud in a playground.

Instead, the bucks and their ladies drove back to London, curled and scented but perhaps a little weary following a ball the previous night. The Derby Stakes to them was just another race. It did achieve brief notoriety in 1788 when the Prince of Wales left his Carlton House residence in London

at 8 a.m. in order to reach the Downs in time to see Sir Thomas and jockey Bill South triumph in the royal colours at 6/5 on.

The town was crowded for the occasion and a Prince's Stand specially built, without which Prinny would have missed a good deal of the running. It was impossible to see more than the last five furlongs on the old 'straight' mile, and, though the distance had been changed in 1784 to a mile and a half on the horseshoe track, the start was still obscured by the woods on Walton Downs.

no matter how brilliant on a straight or flat course, is not a perfect racehorse.

Rickman rightly adds that nine out of ten Derby winners are rattling good horses, not upset by the hubbub of half a million people, and therefore both temperamentally and physically sound and likely to improve the breed; and that is what flat racing is all about.

By his second marriage, Henry Dorling became the stepfather of Isabella Mayson, later Mrs Beeton, the most famous cook of all time. The Dorling family lived in the grandstand, although banished for Derby week to Brighton, where Dorling was also Clerk of the Course.

In 1846, the first major sponsored race was added. The Grand meeting in May by now featured the Craven Stakes for three-year-olds and upwards on the Tuesday, over a mile-and-a-quarter, and a three-year-old event, the Shirley Stakes, over a mile on the same day, together with the Woodcote Stakes for two-year-olds over six furlongs.

The Derby was run on the now traditional Wednesday, a two-year-old seller on Thursday (winner to be sold for £200), and the Oaks on Friday, but Dorling was anxious for a two miles and a quarter handicap event to boost the Spring Meeting, a one day fixture with a mile three-year-old race and an all-age seller, run in mile heats.

News reached Samuel Beeton (no relation), the landlord of a pub in Milk Street, Cheapside, that Dorling was having difficulty finding the prize money for the new race, to be called the Great Metropolitan. Pubs in those days acted as unofficial betting shops and Beeton had no trouble

in raising £300 from his own punters and those in neighbouring ale-houses. The first Great Met, starting in front of the stands with the field running the reverse way of the straight, branching right just before Tattenham Corner and winding across the open Downs to join the course at the mile-and-a-quarter post for the run to home, was won by Chamois.

The race was such a success that another event sponsored by prize money collected in pubs spread its net a little wider, from the city into the suburbs. It was inevitably called the City and Surburban, first run over a mile and a quarter in 1851.

Although these races are of little significance today, for many years the Great Met and the City and Sub, as they were affectionately known to Londoners, were big betting events and the subjects of huge ante-post gambles. The City and Surburban still survives in a shadow of its original form, but the Great Metropolitan was reduced to a mile and a half in 1985, when it became too dangerous to race horses across the Downs.

Royal patronage returned in the late nineteenth century in the not unsubstantial shape of the Prince of Wales, later King Edward VII, who won the Derbies of 1896, 1900 and 1907 with Persimmon, Diamond Jubilee and Minoru, the only horse owned by a reigning monarch to win the premier classic.

It has been fashionable in recent years for National Hunt enthusiasts to 'crab' classic winners on the grounds that they run perhaps no more than four or five times and earn huge sums, while elderly and stout-hearted geldings have to complete the equivalent of several circuits of the M25

AN HISTORIC TURF GROUP. THE PRINCE OF
WALES WITH HIS FIRST DERBY WINNER,
PERSIMMON, RIDDEN BY JOHN WATTS.
RICHARD MARSH, THE TRAINER, IS AT THE
HORSE'S HEAD

BACK AT EPSOM, AFTER THE WAR, AIRBORNE
WON THE 1946 DERBY

of Lord Wigg and the generosity of Stanley Wooton, a crisis was averted.

Former trainer Wooton had acquired the Walton Downs for £35,000 from the old Grandstand Association when the new stands were being financed by the Dorlings in 1925. This land he donated to the Horserace Betting Levy Board, of which Wigg was Chairman, in 1969. Wigg proceeded to purchase Epsom Downs as well for £1,359,000, the whole area being placed under the control of the Board's subsidiary, United Racecourses.

Now it is possible to erect enclosures on the Downs, and charge admission, regulate gypsy encampments and provide Tote and other facilities for the thousands who flock to Epsom by road, rail and helicopter to see who will win the Blue Ribbon of the Turf. Despite the rise in importance of aged European races such as the Arc de Triomphe, the King George VI and The Queen Elizabeth Stakes, competition from the Irish Derby and the recent development of highly-prized American races, the Derby remains the ambition of every breeder, every owner, every lad, every trainer and every jockey; it's quite simply the one they all want to win.

DERBY DAY, 1971

WALTER DORLING

chance of avoiding her and horse, jockey and suffragette all crashed to the ground.

The fact that the King's horse was involved was almost certainly pure chance, although it made a good newspaper story. As Donoghue points out, it would be impossible to single out one horse at racing pace, and Herbert Jones never forgot the look of horror on the girl's face at the moment of impact. He remained convinced that it was not an act of fanaticism, but an accident. However, given Emily Davison's record of militance, the possibility that she acted deliberately must remain.

During the First World War, the course was closed, the Derby and Oaks were run at New-

market and the grandstand became a mil[...] hospital. When Epsom reopened for G[...] Parade's 1919 Derby victory, the old 'stra[...] mile course had gone, chopped off at the [...] furlong start, and the stands were inadequa[...] deal with the brief post-war boom.

The Dorling family were still in comm[...] and decided to build a new stand, which rema[...] this day. Unhappily the boom deflated int[...] misery of the General Strike, and the work[...] had to be bribed with a banquet at the exper[...] Lord Lonsdale, then Senior Steward of the J[...] Club, before the enclosures were in readine[...] Call Boy's Derby in 1927.

The second global conflict of the twe[...] century saw Epsom again under military oc[...] tion, and the Derby and Oaks transferr[...] Newmarket. In the late 1940s the Derby w[...] on Saturday in a bid to prevent absenteei[...] Britain struggled to recover from five years [...] and the bomb-battered grandstand was fr[...] repaired.

But the future of Epsom, home of the w[...] greatest race, had yet to be secured, and th[...] not done until as recently as 1984. The [...] were essentially common land, and whi[...] Epsom and Walton Downs Regulation Act [...] protected the interests of the racecourse an[...] trainers, it also granted free access to the [...] public, who could in theory picnic in the mi[...] the track on Derby Day.

By the mid-sixties, the Act was hopeles[...] of date, given the huge increase in the vol[...] motor traffic and parking requirements. T[...] was due to lapse in 1984, and thanks to the[...]

His attitude to politics changed radically in 1846 when the Prime Minister, Sir Robert Peel, embraced the cause of Free Trade. Lord George promptly formed the Protectionist Party and recruited Benjamin Disraeli as his deputy. He then proceeded to sell his entire racing and bloodstock interests for £10,000. Within two years his Commons campaign had succeeded and it seemed as though the same energy that Bentinck had put into racing would ensure a brilliant parliamentary career; but it was not to be. A few months later he died at the age of forty-six.

Robbed of their guiding spirit, it was not long before the Richmond stables were closed and the animals dispersed. Although both the quality of the racing and prize money levels dropped following Bentinck's death, with the 1862 total of £11,274 being less than half of the 1845 winnings, Goodwood races continued to maintain their popularity.

It was in the 1850s when foreign owners started to make their mark on British racing. One of them was the American, Richard Ten Broeck, who won the 1857 Cesarewitch with Prioress, the first American-bred horse to win a race in England. Prioress went on to finish third in the Goodwood Cup in 1859, and Ten Broeck's Starke won the Goodwood Stakes in the same year, and again in 1861.

Meanwhile the French invaders had also started to make their mark. Jouvence won the Goodwood Cup in 1853, and Monarque was victorious in the 1857 running in the colours of Count Frédéric de Lagrange, later made famous by Monarque's son Gladiateur, Triple Crown

winner in 1865 and known as 'The Avenger of Waterloo'.

Count Frederic, who was based in Normandy, sent his stud to England in 1872 on the outbreak of the Franco-Prussian war. The horses were leased by another Frenchman, Jean-Claude Lefévre, who won ten races at the 1873 Goodwood meeting, including the Goodwood Cup with a three-year-old, Flageolet.

Hostilities over, Lagrange himself returned to Goodwood in 1875 and won seven races; and the stage was set for the appearance of the brilliant Hungarian mare, Kincsem, to take the Goodwood Cup in 1878. Kincsem was never beaten in fifty-four races in five European countries and can be rivalled only by Sceptre and Pretty Polly as the greatest of racemares.

Another famous Hungarian, Prince Gustavus Batthyany, was an intrepid amateur rider still booting home winners at the age of fifty at such long-lost meetings as Croxton Park (Melton Mowbray), Egham and Bedford. He owned Galopin, the Derby winner of 1875, and from Galopin he bred Galliard out of a mare called Mavis; and he also bred St Simon. Galliard was the unwitting cause of his breeder's death, as the eighty-year-old Prince Batthyany failed to survive the pre-race excitement when Galliard was made favourite for the Two Thousand Guineas of 1883. The Prince suffered a heart attack and died as he attempted to ascend the steps to the Jockey Club luncheon room.

For the record, Galliard duly won in the hands of Fred Archer, but more importantly as it was to turn out, the two-year-old St Simon's engage-

FRED ARCHER

ments, including the classics, were made void by the Prince's death under the Rules of Racing at the time.

Purchased by the Duke of Portland for 1,600 guineas when the Batthyany horses came up for sale in July 1883, St Simon made his racecourse debut at Goodwood a few weeks later in the Halnaker Stakes and the Maiden Plate, both of which he won easily under Fred Archer.

Having slaughtered the opposition in his remaining two-year-old races, St Simon achieved the rare distinction of 'carting' Archer on the Newmarket gallops and went on to win the Ascot Gold Cup by twenty lengths. He rounded off his eleven-race career where he began, at Goodwood, by winning the Cup from his two opponents by another twenty lengths, Archer finding it impossible to pull St Simon up until the horse had run himself out.

St Simon was to sire ten classic winners and was quite probably the finest colt ever to race. Goodwood had reason to be proud of his exploits on the springy downland turf, untouched for generations except for the last half mile which was considered by the redoubtable Bentinck to be not sufficiently resilient in hot weather and relaid under his instructions in the 1840s.

By the 'Gay Nineties', the meeting had become the fashionable way to relax after the arduous formalities of the London social season, and at the turn of the century F.H. Bayles, in his fascinating *Racecourse Atlas*, is eulogising:

'Everything here is done sans ceremonie, and the al fresco luncheon parties in the avenue of tall spreading beeches may be described as excelling a

ABOVE, THE TRUNDLE HILL BEFORE IT WAS
ENCLOSED, AND LEFT, IN 1975

colossal Cafe Chantant, or the Champeaux in the Place de la Bourse, on a very large scale; while the entire place is open to all, to brush shoulders with Royalties (when present), Peers, Peeresses, Ambassadors, Ministers of State, administrators of the law, the leading lights of literature, science and finance, all forgetting, pro tem., their interest in Imperial State'.

Nonetheless, formal morning dress, as at Ascot, was de rigeur until 1906, when King Edward VII turned up in a lounge suit, observing that Goodwood was 'a garden party with racing tacked on'. This was later bowdlerised into a supposed royal reference to Goodwood's 'garden party atmosphere', which is not quite the same thing.

The twentieth century has seen some epic races, notably Old Orkney's victory over Brown Jack in 1929. These two superb stayers fought out the Goodwood Cup neck and neck at level weights over the last three furlongs, Old Orkney prevailing by a short head. It was considered by those who saw it to be one of the most magnificent long-distance races of all time. Brown Jack recompensed his many supporters by winning the Cup in 1930 at 9/4 on for Steve Donoghue.

1947 found a different sort of drama, and typical of the post-war racing boom produced by returning ex-servicemen with money to burn. The crowds were huge, and so were the traffic jams which were made worse by a series of crashes.

Noel Murless was to become the doyen of English trainers, with nineteen classic winners to his credit, and was already the leading northern trainer. None of this was to be of any help when the

horsebox, conveying Murless's Steward's Cup runner, Closeburn, from his Hambleton, Yorkshire, stables via an overnight stop at Weyhill, was caught in a hopeless snarl-up in the narrow lanes of Singleton, north of the course.

Quick thinking by Mrs Gwen, now Lady, Murless, brought Closeburn from his horsebox onto the track after a two-mile jog, just in time to be saddled and win the Steward's Cup, by a neck, ridden by Gordon Richards and carrying the then record-breaking weight for a three-year-old of 8st 10lb.

But perhaps the real hero of post-war Goodwood was the Irish-bred Predominate. After a successful career on the flat, also winning twice over hurdles, he was bought by Jim Joel with a view to making Predominate a top-class hurdler. When the gelding showed that he did not really like hurdling, Mr Joel decided that Predominate should revert to the flat.

Trained by Ted Leader and ridden by Eph Smith, Predominate won the Goodwood Stakes in three successive years, his victories in 1959 and 1960 being under 9st 5lb. He also won the Queen Alexandra Stakes at Ascot in 1960 and the Goodwood Cup in 1961, at the age of nine.

This was Predominate's last race. With a mile to go, Smith felt that the horse had broken down, and he was prepared to surrender. Predominate would have nothing of it, and battled on to win by a short head.

Today, Goodwood stands at a crossroads. The Cup, the Stakes and the Steward's Cup all bear witness to the richness of the past, together with the Sussex Stakes and the Nassau Stakes. More

HAYMAKING AT GOODWOOD, 1930

recently founded races such as the Gordon Stakes (for me one of the best events at the meeting) and the Richmond Stakes have also stood the test of time. However, in common with other mid-season top two-year-old races, such as the Coventry Stakes, since modern breeding methods favour precocity the flow of future classic winners, formerly a feature of the Richmond, has been stemmed. Janette (Oaks), Pommern and Manna (Derby), Columbo (2,000 Guineas), Mahmoud (Derby) and Palestine (2,000 Guineas) all displayed their ability at Goodwood.

The quality of racing has been maintained; other qualities have not. The grandstand, opened in 1980, was always too small for Goodwood's modern needs and although improvements are planned, the course may have become a victim of its own success; over-commercialisation may possibly have contributed to the ugly scenes of violence more typical of eighteenth-century racegoing, which have marred the beauty of the Sussex countryside in recent times. ∎

PREDOMINATE POWERS HOME TO WIN THE
GOODWOOD STAKES, 1959

KEMPTON

'The spectacle at Waterloo Station, as train after train is despatched to the scene of the action, much resembles that to be witnessed on the forenoon of a Derby or Ascot Cup day, whilst at the termination of the ride by train, visitors find themselves in the Stands or Paddock almost immediately after quitting the railway carriage. Everywhere prevails the most perfect order, and the best of possible taste. The shrubberies and flower beds are arranged with exquisite view to effect, the bands that discourse sweet music between races are the best to be obtained, and on a sunny afternoon in spring or summer KEMPTON PARK is quite a fairyland of horse racing.'

EULOGISING ON to add, that even if a shower should mar the afternoon, no harm would be done to 'the toilet of the ladies' as they could walk to their stations under complete shelter, the *Racing Illustrated Magazine* thus described the delights of Kempton Park in 1896.

The particular wizard who had waved his wand and conjured up the 'fairyland of horse racing' was a hard-headed business man, S.H. Hyde. Hyde was the descendant of Lancashire textile barons, and the son of a solicitor practising in Ashton-under-Lyne. His political ambitions found him as a Tory agent in Bristol at a time when parliamentary fortunes fluctuated between Benjamin Disraeli and William Gladstone; for all Dizzy's flamboyance, the Conservatives never held a clear majority in the Commons between 1846 and 1874, and doubtless the Ballot Act introducing secret voting for all elections proved the last straw for a hard-working agent.

Hyde had already become a student of racecourse management, at Bristol, and on a fine day approaching the mid-summer of 1872, Mr Hyde took his wife on a steamer trip down the Thames to Hampton Court; there he decided on a carriage drive in the country.

The Hydes were staying in London for Derby week, and while history does not record whether or not they backed champion jockey Charlie Maidment to win his first Derby on Cremorne, it is certain that Mr Hyde spotted an estate agent's sign outside the Manor and Park of Kempton, advertising the property for sale or lease.

Alighting from his carriage, Hyde was delighted with what he found: a family-sized Victorian house built on the site of an eleventh-century hunting lodge, a lake with good fishing, and four hundred acres in all, ideal flat land on which to build a racecourse.

Doubtless the estate agent's details of the property would have informed Mr Hyde that Kempton Park is mentioned in the Domesday Book of 1086. It was then the home of Robert, Earl of Mortain and almost certainly a reward for services rendered to the Conqueror.

Henry III built a hunting seat around 1250 and stocked the park with deer to provide a pleasant day's sport en route to Windsor. Henry VIII followed suit, though his daughter Elizabeth as Queen leased the manor to William Killigrew. The park became a seat for a series of country squires until Thomas Barnett leased the house and grounds to S.H. Hyde in 1872.

Hyde in turn leased part of the estate to the

S. H. HYDE

THE PROCESSION FROM THE PADDOCK LED BY THUNDERSTOR...

newly formed Kempton Park Racecourse Company of which he was Secretary. On 18th July, 1878, Kempton opened the gates to the public for the first time. It was a 'drawing-room' course, based on neighbouring Sandown's success in catering for the up-market punter, providing for female racegoers and making them feel both wanted and safe, while excluding the ruffians, who then as now, were the plague of sporting events.

The Inauguration Plate of £250 was the first event decided over the new Sunbury course. Fifteen went to post for this six-furlong race including The Mandarin, who was to win the Royal Hunt Cup in 1879. Conceding sixteen pounds, he just failed to catch Dunkenny, trained by John Porter and ridden by George Fordham, the fourteen times champion jockey who never allowed his fondness for gin and port wine to diminish his equal thirst for winners. Fordham made all in his best 'kidding' style to win on Dunkenny and this victory was greatly to assist the resumption of his career after a brief and premature retirement at the court of Bacchus.

Although the Inauguration Plate was over six furlongs, it was run on the Kempton mile track. At this time the infield, including the straight six-furlong course, was enclosed and used for hare coursing, a sport close to the heart of S.H. Hyde, who kept a kennel of twenty-four dogs, including Ballnageigh, beaten in the final of the Waterloo Cup. The straight course remained unused until 1884, when coursing was abandoned as the cost of obtaining hares had become excessive. No doubt there are a few such unhappy creatures around today who wish the same market forces could apply

MINTING FULL OF RUNNING CAME OUT & WON EASILY BY THREE LENGTHS

MINTING AFTER THE RACE

MINTING, WINNER OF THE GRAND JUBILEE
HANDICAP, 1888

to them in these more benevolent times.

In 1887, the Grand Jubilee Handicap was run on 7th May, to mark Queen Victoria's fiftieth year on the throne. The winner was Bendigo, hero of the first Eclipse Stakes the year before. Now a seven-year-old, 'Bendy' had taken on the kind of mantle of popular esteem inherited by horses like Brown Jack, and nowadays usually reserved for all-conquering steeplechasers.

Humping 9st 7lbs and ridden by John Watts over the mile course (the distance became ten furlongs in 1900 but reverted to a mile in 1979), Bendigo started favourite at 4/1 and won by three-quarters of a length, from Martley and Tyrone. According to *Racing Illustrated*, 'People shouted themselves hoarse, and struggled to get near the victor, who, if we remember rightly, received the reward of an apple, besides being greatly caressed'.

Robert Vyner's Minting, trained by Matt Dawson and, like The Bard, unlucky enough to be foaled in the same year as Ormonde, did even better in 1888, winning easily by three lengths carrying ten stone, which remains a record for the race.

The first dual winner was Victor Wild, in 1885 and '86. Owned by a London publican, Tom Worton, who had bought the horse out of a seller at Portsmouth for £330, Victor Wild started at 20/1 for his 1885 success under 8st 4lb, although Worton's customers had touted the victualler's confidence all over London.

Following Victor Wild's second victory with a steadier of 9st 7lb, the bookies wept as the sporting writers compared the joys of Kempton with the bad old days of suburban racing. It seems that Bromley had a ramshackle stand behind which many little coups common to the suburban Turf were arranged, that Streatham had to be circuited interminably before two miles could be completed, West Drayton was of 'impious memory', and Lillie Bridge beyond description.

The Jubilee was plundered in later years by those two master trainers, Atty Persse and Persse's former pupil, Cecil Boyd-Rochfort, who both won the race six times. The victory of the Persse-trained Bachelor's Double in 1911 was something of a miracle. Although Atty Persse operated in a cloud of secrecy which would have been the envy of James Bond, an inspired leak revealed to the world outside the bleak confines of Chattis Hill that all the horses had been coughing. Accordingly, Bachelor's Double, winner of the Irish Derby in 1909 and the Royal Hunt Cup under 8st 4lb in 1910 was allowed to start at 100/7 and win by four lengths like the certainty he was. Jockey Steve Donoghue modestly reported that the stable had 'a really good win'.

Royal Tara's victory in 1947 was even more remarkable, as the Irish Two Thousand Guineas winner of 1946 was propelled home to a neck victory from Claro, the Irish Guineas winner of '47, by a sharp nip in the quarters from the French Challenger, Epi d'Or VII, goaded into this action by his Gallic rider's over-enthusiastic use of the whip.

Epi d'Or VII would doubtless have found a piece of his cowboy jockey even more satisfying; as it was he finished third to Royal Tara, whose rider, the former champion apprentice Tommy Gosling, was suitably happy with the outcome.

FIRE DESTROYED MOST OF THE MEMBERS'
STAND, 1932

Today, the Jubilee, like the City and Suburban and the Great Metropolitan, is something of a light of former years, a victim of the patterns of modern racing, but its place in Kempton's history is assured for ever.

The course's early popularity ensured a good allocation of Bank Holiday fixtures, and since 1895 the Queen's Prize, a two-mile handicap usually featuring a few race-fit hurdlers, has been a standing dish for the vast Easter crowds. The Rosebery Stakes, over the mile-and-a-quarter Jubilee course, was first run in 1932 and proved an equal success.

By now, S.H. Hyde had been succeeded by his son Walter as Secretary, and Kempton had survived the 1914-18 war as a military transport depot. 1932 was to be a dramatic year. Fire broke out on September 28th and destroyed most of the Members' Stand, the Grill Room and the Tattersalls Bar. The architects recommended that the October meeting should be abandoned. Having received assurance that their luncheon could be served in the weighing-room, the stewards allowed the racing to proceed. The public sensibly stayed away and the course was closed for a £100,000 rebuild not completed until 1934, but Kempton re-opened in May 1933, in time for Columbo to win the Imperial Produce Stakes with Steve Donoghue up.

Sadly, it was only a few years before the storm clouds of war were gathering again and the stands were soon occupied by troops. The course was fenced off, and became a major reception centre for Italian and German prisoners of war. The private station, which had been the pride of S.H. Hyde

and the London and South Western Railway, made Kempton ideal for the purpose. It was a far cry from the genteel drawing-room atmosphere of the 1870s as the Italian prisoners in uniforms more suited to the male chorus of a tatty revival of 'The Desert Song', were shepherded along the covered paths which once protected the 'toilets of the ladies'.

When the course was de-requisitioned on 1st September, 1946, the prospects were bleak. An annual rent of £6,000 during the war had not covered the upkeep, and the damage to the interior of the buildings, to the last three furlongs of the track and to the paddock was considerable.

The cost was estimated at £73,575 16s. 4d, the odd 16/4d being the cost of returning to the authorities a prisoner found happily doing his washing in one of the grandstand towers two weeks after his comrades had been repatriated.

Rebuilding was to continue for some time, but by Saturday, 5th April, 1947, Kempton was ready to face postwar Britain with the traditional Easter meeting. The crowds of ex-servicemen in their demob suits flocked to spend their war gratuities, and the 1955 Easter fixture attracted a record crowd of 54,000. Walter Hyde, who had served Kempton for fifty-seven years, died in 1951, and was succeeded by his son Henry. The future looked deceptively secure.

During this period, the metropolitan racegoer was decidedly spoilt for choice. The delights of Kempton, Sandown and Hurst Park were all within easy reach on the 'rattler' from Waterloo, while Epsom and Lingfield were only a little further out of town, and the Londoners' very own

PICTURESQUE ACTION DURING THE COVENTRY
PLATE, 1934

course, the much loved Ally Pally (Alexandra Palace) was only six miles from Charing Cross.

As we sipped our wine in pleasant company, enjoying sun-dappled days and warm evenings at our favourite courses, we hardly noticed the beating of wings in the skies above our heads. But sure enough the vultures were circling, in the guise of the property developers.

Hurst Park was the first to be gobbled up, and Sandown only survived after a Government enquiry at ministerial level. The threat to Kempton was at first caused by pressure to sell the by now three-hundred acre estate for valuable gravel workings. At this stage, a sale was averted, but as the gravel was extracted over a period from the mid 1960s, Kempton declined both in the quality of racing and the maintenance of the course and the facilities.

The civil engineering and building firm of Taylor Woodrow made a bid for Kempton in 1969, but racing was preserved when the millionaire racehorse owner and philanthropist, Sir David Robinson, topped the offer and purchased the site for £756,000.

It was Robinson's idea to turn Kempton Park into a large leisure complex which could be used on non-racing days. He paid the inevitable penalty for being ahead of his time, and planning permission was refused, but he generously re-sold the property to the Levy Board for the price which he had incurred and control passed to the Board's subsidiary, United Racecourses, which was already administering Sandown and Epsom.

After over ninety years, the Hyde dynasty's work was done, although Henry Hyde continued

as Secretary. George Boon took over as Clerk of the Course in 1973 when, in his own words, 'Kempton was right down and almost out'. One of the first jobs was to build a new stable block adjacent to the paddock. The old Victorian stables behind the back stretch presented a hazard for jockeys negotiating the open ditch which was not immediately apparent to the 'riders' in the stand. In the words of Tim Fitzgeorge-Parker, 'As you approached the fence your horse's ears went backwards and forwards. He wasn't thinking of the obstacle, but of his nice warm stable. It was a nasty feeling for the rider.'

It was at this ditch that Dunkirk was killed in his valiant challenge to Arkle in the King George VI Chase in 1965. Although it is not my intention to discuss National Hunt racing, it is fundamental to the Kempton story, for there can be little doubt that it was the winter sport which pulled the course through the darkest days, with the capacity Boxing Day crowds cheering home the likes of Mill House, Titus Oates, The Dikler, Pendil and Captain Christy.

The Easter meetings could hardly fail. The odd novelty helped, such as the Goya Stakes, the first modern race for women riders, run on 6th May, 1972 and won by Meriel Tufnell on her mother's Scorched Earth at 50/1. So, along with Mill Reef's victory in the 1970 Imperial Stakes, the flat race flag was kept from drooping too low. But if Kempton had succumbed, I venture to suggest that no-one would have been more disappointed than National Hunt racing's finest patron, Her Majesty Queen Elizabeth, the Queen Mother.

As Queen Elizabeth, she won the 1950 King

Kempton

GERMAN P.O.W.'S AT KEMPTON PARK, 1945

THE IMPERIAL STAKES WON BY MILL REEF, 1970

Kempton

George VI Chase, named in honour of the King in his coronation year, 1937, with Manicou; a string of royal victories with horses including Escalus, The Rip, Makaldar and Game Spirit ensured the continuation of a regal link with Kempton which began when Fairplay won the Royal Handicap Steeplechase in the colours of the Prince of Wales, later King Edward VII, in April 1882.

The filly, Geheimniss, was the first flat race winner for the Prince when she won the Kempton Park Cambridgeshire Trial in 1883. Sadly, Kempton was also the scene of his last victory, when Witch of the Air won the Spring Two-Year-Old Plate on 6th May, 1910 and the news was conveyed to the King on his deathbed. His Majesty's Derby winner, Minoru, was due to contest the Jubilee the following day, but naturally the meeting was abandoned as the nation went into mourning.

Perhaps never quite as popular as the sister course at Sandown, Kempton nevertheless celebrated the 1978 centenary with a confidence for the future few would have shared twenty years before. Today the course is thriving again with good-class three-year-old races, the Masaka Stakes for fillies and the Easter Stakes for colts run over a mile at the traditional Bank Holiday fixture, in addition to the historic Queen's Prize and the Rosebery Stakes. The September Stakes, a Group Three event for three-year-olds and upwards, brings a touch of quality to the autumn season, while the dear old Jubilee marches on, as a soldier of the Queen should, recruited over a century ago and still on active service. ■

LINGFIELD

SINCE THE days of Charles II and sweet Nell of old Drury, there has been an affinity between racing and the theatre, although few have been able to combine the diverse talents required to reach the heights in both spheres.

One who did was the late Tom Walls. He filled the Aldwych Theatre for years in the twenties and thirties when he co-starred with Ralph Lynn and Robertson 'Bunny' Hare in a series of farces by Ben Travers. A keen amateur rider, Walls used the proceeds from his theatrical success to open a small yard at Epsom. The smack of greasepaint was never far away; Teddy Underdown, later a champion amateur rider who partnered the dual Champion hurdler, National Spirit, in his flat races, rode out regularly for Stanley Wooton's string on the Epsom Downs before repairing to the West End to star in Noel Coward musicals.

In the spring of 1932, Walls had charge of April the Fifth, unplaced as a two-year-old but the winner of a maiden event at Gatwick at three. In the same year, the Clerk of the Course at Lingfield, Fred Wilmot, inaugurated the Derby Trial Stakes at the track which so strongly resembled Epsom in conformation that it seemed a natural venue for such an event.

Success was immediate for Walls and Wilmot. April the Fifth was unfancied in the thirteen-strong field for the £378 prize; other runners included the subsequent St Leger winner Firdaussi, Silvermere, who went on to win the Ascot Gold Vase, and Foxhunter who was to win the Doncaster Cup, but April the Fifth won by six lengths.

Still not taken seriously as a Derby candidate by the public, who may have been deterred by the comedic reputation of the owner-trainer, April and Fifth was allowed to start at 100/6 for the premier classic and won by a comfortable three-quarters of a length from Dastur. Winning jockey Fred Lane was steering the first Epsom-trained winner for ninety-four years and no horse prepared on the Downs has won the Derby since.

The Lingfield Derby Trial has never looked back as the key pointer to Epsom success, rivalled only by a classic race, the Two Thousand Guineas. Up to the time of writing, no fewer than seven future Derby winners have demonstrated their Epsom potential at the course always known as 'Lovely Lingfield'.

Lingfield

LINGFIELD, 1975

Also on the card on that significant day in Surrey was the Open Club Welter Stakes for gentlemen riders. Many were true amateurs in those less cynical times. Prince Aly Khan had ridden his father's Taj Ud Din into third place in 1931 and in 1932 the late Lord Carnarvon, not unfairly described at the time as a latter-day Regency buck, won on Kiang with the thespian Teddy Underdown out with the washing on Friar Bacon. Carnarvon won again on Knight of Lorn in 1933, when Tom Walls was unplaced on Tibetan Prince.

Fred Wilmot lost no time in founding an Oaks Trial, and although not enjoying the same instant success as the colts' event, the fillies' race has indicated Sleeping Partner, Ginevra, Juliette Marny and Aliysa as winners on Epsom's Ladies' Day.

Racing at Lingfield started humbly enough as a minor National Hunt meeting in November 1890, and the opening race, a selling hunters flat race, was won by an animal rejoicing in the name of Old Tatt. Despite this inauspicious beginning, Lingfield attracted enough support to warrant flat racing in 1894, and HRH the Prince of Wales attended the first meeting on 16th May.

Lingfield jogged along happily enough as a pleasant country course until Wilmot's 1932 breakthrough put the Surrey track firmly on the racing map. After twenty-four years' service, Fred

Lingfield

Wilmot retired in 1939 as Lingfield became a prisoner-of-war camp and it fell to one of racing's finest administrators, Major John Crocker Bulteel, later Sir John, to restore the course and buildings in 1946, before handing over to Peter Beckwith-Smith.

Major Beckwith-Smith was a grandson of J.B. Leigh, who in 1927 was responsible for the layout of the course and stands very much as they are today. By 1974 the Beckwith-Smith family came to the sad conclusion that Lingfield was no longer viable for a private company. The bookmaking firm of Ladbrokes purchased the course for £500,000 and were allowed to operate after a certain amount of heart-searching by the mandarins of the Home Office. They didn't entirely approve of bookie-fellows running a racetrack, but gave reluctant consent after realising that refusal would have ensured the closure of the course and that John Hughes was not a man to compromise with any employer.

Hughes ran Lingfield with his customary inspiration until Ladbrokes sold out to Ron Muddle in 1982, who in turn passed the ownership to Leisure Investments for £7,000,000 in September 1988, but not before the course had been transformed. Muddle carried out extensive drainage works to alleviate the constant abandonments due to wet weather, and widened the 'Tattenham Corner' bend into the straight. A new story was added to the middle grandstand, with twelve private boxes, the Eclipse stand facing down the course was extended, and a pavilion for five hundred guests built to utilise the course's facilities for corporate entertainment on non-racing as well as racing days.

Today, Lingfield is the only course in Britain to have received consent from the Levy Board to lay down an all-weather track, a consent which includes a £1,500,000 subsidy towards a £3,800,000 project which should be in operation by autumn 1989. But behind all this space-age stuff which the Romans pre-empted two thousand years ago without the benefit of a Senate grant, lies a piquant memory.

On 16th October, 1920, a diminutive sixteen year old apprentice jockey walked an animal called Clock Work from Lingfield station to the course after a journey from Martin Hartigan's yard at Ogbourne Maisey and went on to guide Clock Work into fourth place in a twenty-one strong field for the October Nursery Handicap. The apprentice was having his first ride in public, and weighed out at 6st 9lb with a 5lb allowance deducted; his name was Gordon Richards. ■

LINGFIELD, 1966

NEWBURY

IN 1903 Mr F.H. Bayles wrote, or as he put it himself 'fully described' a *Race Course Atlas of Great Britain and Ireland*. Produced under the patronage of King Edward VII, it is a definitive work and although at the time Newbury racecourse was little more than a glint in John Porter's eye, Bayles's comments on the proposed new track are worth recording.

'If the Calendar will admit of another new fixture to its already congested list [there were actually seventy-three courses in 1903, excluding hunt fixtures, compared to fifty-nine today] I know of no site more suitable for a racecourse than that introduced by a syndicate of influential gentlemen, with the popular trainer of Kingsclere, Mr John Porter as a practical guiding rein, together with sixty training establishments within short distances, having 1,500 horses in daily training. It may be safe to assume that a very hopeful future is in store for Newbury. The stewards of the Jockey Club have intention to grant fixtures for 1905. The proposed site is on a very fine area of 300 acres of good grass country, adjoining the copse known as the Aviary, half a mile from Newbury Station.'

Going on to describe proposals for such essential matters as a railway siding and horse dock, stable lads' accommodation and the conformation of the course, Bayles ends, 'May the meeting have the reward it will deserve'.

Well, eventually it did and Newbury has been established almost from the beginning as one of the top flat courses in the country, but there were a few battles to be fought before the rewards could be reaped.

Bayles's comments on the congested fixture

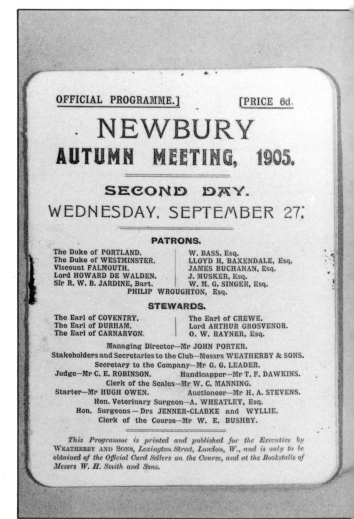

OFFICIAL PROGRAMME.]   [PRICE 6d.

NEWBURY
AUTUMN MEETING, 1905.

SECOND DAY.
WEDNESDAY, SEPTEMBER 27.

PATRONS.

The Duke of PORTLAND.
The Duke of WESTMINSTER.
Viscount FALMOUTH.
Lord HOWARD DE WALDEN.
Sir R. W. B. JARDINE, Bart.

W. BASS, Esq.
LLOYD H. BAXENDALE, Esq.
JAMES BUCHANAN, Esq.
J. MUSKER, Esq.
W. M. G. SINGER, Esq.

PHILIP WROUGHTON, Esq.

STEWARDS.

The Earl of COVENTRY.
The Earl of DURHAM.
The Earl of CARNARVON.

The Earl of CREWE.
Lord ARTHUR GROSVENOR.
O. W. RAYNER, Esq.

Managing Director—Mr JOHN PORTER.
Stakeholders and Secretaries to the Club—Messrs WEATHERBY & SONS.
Secretary to the Company—Mr G. G. LEADER.
Judge—Mr C. E. ROBINSON.   Handicapper—Mr T. F. DAWKINS.
Clerk of the Scales—Mr W. C. MANNING.
Starter—Mr HUGH OWEN.   Auctioneer—Mr H. A. STEVENS.
Hon. Veterinary Surgeon—A. WHEATLEY, Esq.
Hon. Surgeons—Drs JENNER-CLARKE and WYLLIE.
Clerk of the Course—Mr W. E. BUSHBY.

This Programme is printed and published for the Executive by WEATHERBY AND SONS, *Lexington Street, London, W., and is only to be obtained of the Official Card Sellers on the Course, and at the Bookstalls of Messrs* W. H. Smith *and Sons.*

Twenty first Anniversary
of the first Newbury meeting

Directors' Luncheon

Thursday Sept 24 1925

Consommé St. Hubert

Suprême de Sole Héloïse

Poulet sauté à l'Hongroise
Selle de Pré-salé rôtie
Pommes de Terre Mousseline
Haricots Verts à la Crème

Viandes Froides

Poires Florida
Friandines à la Galloise

Dessert

Directors' Room
Newbury Race-course Co., Ltd.
Thursday, September 24th, 1925.

Bertram & Co., Ltd.,
Caterers.

OFFICIAL PROGRAMME.]   [PRICE 6d.

NEWBURY
AUTUMN MEETING, 1905.

FIRST DAY.
TUESDAY, SEPTEMBER 26TH.

PATRONS.

The Duke of PORTLAND.
The Duke of WESTMINSTER.
Viscount FALMOUTH.
Lord HOWARD DE WALDEN.
Sir R. W. B. JARDINE, Bart.

W. BASS, Esq.
LLOYD H. BAXENDALE, Esq.
JAMES BUCHANAN, Esq.
J. MUSKER, Esq.
W. M. G. SINGER, Esq.

PHILIP WROUGHTON, Esq.

STEWARDS.

The Earl of COVENTRY.
The Earl of DURHAM.
The Earl of CARNARVON.

The Earl of CREWE.
Lord ARTHUR GROSVENOR.
O. W. RAYNER, Esq.

Managing Director—Mr JOHN PORTER.
Stakeholders and Secretaries to the Club—Messrs WEATHERBY & SONS.
Secretary to the Company—Mr G. G. LEADER.
Judge—Mr C. E. ROBINSON.   Handicapper—Mr T. F. DAWKINS.
Clerk of the Scales—Mr W. C. MANNING.
Starter—Mr HUGH OWEN.   Auctioneer—Mr H. A. STEVENS.
Hon. Veterinary Surgeon—A. WHEATLEY, Esq.
Hon. Surgeons—Drs JENNER-CLARKE and WYLLIE.
Clerk of the Course—Mr W. E. BUSHBY.

*This Programme is printed and published for the Executive by
WEATHERBY AND SONS, Lexington Street, London, W., and is only to be
obtained of the Official Card Sellers on the Course, and at the Bookstalls of
Messrs W. H. Smith and Sons.*

NEWBURY'S FIRST RACECARD, 26th SEPTEMBER,
1905, AND FOUNDER JOHN PORTER

list were to be proved prophetic; when John Porter laid his final plans before them, the Jockey Club rejected them on the grounds that there were too many courses already. Porter was a man who had trained eighteen winners for the King when the latter was Prince of Wales and the mythology has it that Porter, emerging from his meeting at the Jockey Club rooms feeling thoroughly unwanted, bumped into no less a personage than the monarch himself, as Edward VII was strolling along Newmarket High Street.

The trainer explained his problems to his former patron, and the King told Porter to see him the next day, when he suggested that a fresh application to the Stewards might be more favourably received. Whatever the truth of the casual encounter in the High Street, Porter was duly granted his licence to operate the new racecourse.

It was not to be the first time racing had been staged at Newbury, as meetings were held annually on nearby Enbourne Heath in Regency days under the patronage of Lord Carnarvon of Highclere Castle, but it appears that these were rather ill-organised affairs and the card included donkey races.

The founder of modern Newbury had been born in 1838 at Rugeley in Staffordshire, where the family doctor was William Palmer, the infamous poisoner. Surviving the ministrations of Dr Palmer, John Porter was apprenticed to John Barham Day in Sussex, and commenced a brief riding career enjoying his first success on Overreach at Brighton in 1855.

However, he had only just over twenty rides all told and made his final appearance in the saddle on Carmel in the 1858 Derby.

Porter commenced training in 1863 at Findon, moving to Kingsclere in 1868. From here he sent out a staggering total of twenty-three classic winners, including seven Derby triumphs, and during an outstanding career trained the winners of 1,063 races worth £720,021.

Contemplating his retirement at the turn of the century, Porter decided that the fine piece of land which he had had ample time to study as he frequently travelled to London from Newbury on the adjoining Great Western Railway Line, would make an ideal racecourse. Forming a syndicate with the owner of the land, Mr L.H. Baxendale, Porter prepared to retire from training and the first Newbury meeting was held on Tuesday, 26th September, 1905 before a crowd of 15,000 racegoers.

The going was soft on the bed of lush turf nestling on the drift of river and valley gravel overlying the foundation of London clay which constitutes the geology of Newbury. Twenty-eight runners went to post for the first race, the five-furlong Whatcombe Handicap worth £160, a little before two o'clock. The honour of riding the 100/7 winner, Copper King, went to Pretty Polly's original jockey Charlie Trigg, known in the weighing room as 'Hellfire Jack' on account of some dashing exploits around the trappy turns of Epsom and Chester.

It was no surprise to the vast crowd that the only favourite of the day to oblige, Theodore in the nursery seller, was trained by Atty Persse, since the man who was to prepare that flier The Tetrarch

230

MINORU, WITH JOCKEY HERBERT JONES, 1909

for his undefeated seven-race career in 1913, had already made a name for himself in Ireland as a shrewd trainer of juveniles and an intrepid gambler.

Persse trained four more winners at the two-day meeting to net £953 in prize money and Lord Carnarvon won three races on the first day, including the £1,375 Inaugural Handicap over one and a half miles with the 100/12 shot Missovaja.

But perhaps the greatest cheers were reserved for the man whose brainchild had finally come to pass. John Porter trained Zealous to win the £100 Regulation Plate, the last race on Wednesday's card. Porter won £10,644 in stakes in his final season as a trainer, but it is doubtful if many of his

successes gave him as much pleasure as the humble Regulation Plate.

John Porter continued as Managing Director of Newbury during his retirement and died in 1922 at the age of eighty-four, leaving Newbury as his finest legacy to the sport which he loved so much.

A programme not dissimilar from today's was quickly established. The Spring Cup, of £1,250 and originally over one mile, was inaugurated in 1906 and won by Succory, and the Greenham Stakes was established in the same year, swiftly becoming a recognised Two Thousand Guineas trial. In 1909 Edward VII's Minoru defeated the odds-on favourite Valens despite the pessimism of his Royal connections following a poor two-year-old season. It is said that before the Greenham, the King's racing manager, Lord Marcus Beresford, considered that Minoru would be overweighted with 7st 4lb in the Steward's Cup. Minoru not only won the Greenham under 9st 10lb but took the Guineas and the Derby as well, ridden by Herbert Jones.

1906 also saw the first running of the Autumn Cup over two miles and a further furlong, victory going to Colonel Tom Kirkwood's The White Knight in the hands of the American jockey 'Skeets' Martin. As The White Knight was to go on to win the Ascot Gold Cup twice, plus the Goodwood and Coronation Cups, it could be said that Newbury was proving to be an excellent trial ground for older horses as well.

The Summer Cup over one-and-a-half miles was also destined to attract some first-class stayers, with Tangiers winning the Ascot Gold Cup in 1920 and Santorb emulating the feat in 1925 both following victories in the Summer Cup. But before those days of peace, Newbury had to deal with the rigours of the Great War.

Racing came to a halt after Aboukir had won the Autumn Cup in 1916 and the course became successively a prisoner-of-war camp, a Munitions Inspection Depot, a hay dispersal depot and finally a tank testing and repair park.

However, the track itself and the original buildings designed and erected by the architect W.C. Stephens emerged relatively unscathed and the turnstiles started to click again in 1919 as Newbury enjoyed the postwar boom, albeit short-lived and ending in the General Strike of 1926. However, neither the strike nor the economic

stagnation of the thirties affected the continuing prosperity of Newbury in the era between the wars when no fewer than twenty-five courses were forced to close.

On the outbreak of World War II, parts of the course were requisitioned but racing struggled on until the summer of 1941. Indeed, it was suggested that the 1940 substitute Derby should be run at Newbury but as the British Expeditionary Force were evacuated from Dunkirk and the war began in earnest, the classic event was switched to Newmarket.

In 1942, the US Armed Forces arrived at Newbury and the course became the site of a main American supply depot. The turf so beloved of John Porter was buried beneath concrete and thirty-five miles of railway lines; the stables were occupied by prisoners of war and the Members' Bar became an Officers' mess.

As racing resumed in the relaxed atmosphere of postwar Britain, Newbury missed out. While millions flocked to Epsom Downs for the 1946 Derby, Geoffrey Freer, one of racing's finest administrators of the period, waited patiently for the Marshall Plan, otherwise known as the Lease and Lend Agreement, to enable the Ministry of Supply to find a fresh home for the immense amount of military hardware cluttering Newbury.

It was June 1947 before the course was released back into civilian hands. The task facing Freer was enormous, but the man whose motto was that 'racing is meant to be fun' was undaunted.

Slowly the vast sea of cementation was cleared, the straight five-furlong course was relaid from the produce of a turf nursery put down in 1944, and a

Newbury

THE KING AND QUEEN AT NEWBURY TO SEE
LIMELIGHT WIN THE SPRING CUP, 1933

nearby housing development supplied the remainder. By 1949, three years after most other tracks put into mothballs by the war were up and running, Newbury was open to the public once again, and racing resumed on All Fools' Day.

But there were long-term advantages. The original back straight was actually a dog-leg, and this was straightened in the process of re-turfing while the bends were made so gentle as to be almost non-existent to the horse, and negotiable at full gallop.

Inevitably, this has made Newbury one of the fairest courses in the country, although good jockeyship is essential. The late Sir Gordon Richards, the finest jockey I have ever seen and the best 'kidder' since George Fordham, loved Newbury and stole many a race he should have lost by

the exercise of superb judgement, as his rivals went too soon or came too late into the straight.

Newbury has certainly been blessed with inspired management, and Geoffrey Freer was backed by John and Frank Osgood, an uncle and nephew who succeeded each other as racecourse managers, and followed by Charles Toller as Clerk of the Course, a post which he still holds today.

Newbury also boasts a fine steeplechasing course and an excellent National Hunt programme. After Ascot it is probably the best course in the South, with a top class series of races including the Greenham, the Fred Darling, the John Porter and the Lockinge Stakes, the Mill Reef Stakes, the Horris Hill and the St Simon Stakes. ∎

233

SANDOWN

'How pleasant once more to find ourselves within the Sandown Club enclosure, under a genial sky, with all the well-known surroundings of pretty women, good luncheon and good sport.'

SO REPORTED the correspondent of *Baily's Magazine* in 1879, and it is hard to quarrel with that description of Sandown today, even if income tax is a little higher than the 2d in the pound levied in the 1870s.

In the words of F.H. Bayles, the undersoil of the course consists of 'lower Bagshot sands'. Doubtless for this reason, the original name of the area just to the west of Esher village was Sandon. In the time of King John the land was cultivated by the monks of an Augustine Priory. Aided by the patronage of one William Percy, whose wife was buried in the grounds, the Priory prospered and acquired fresh lands as far afield as Dunsfold, Chessington, Tadworth, Walton and Kingston.

Unhappily for the brethren, the religious life was not compatible with the demands of Mammon; the venture failed financially by 1300, and the few survivors were wiped out by the plague in 1338. Attempts to revive the order at Sandon were negated by the Black Death in 1349.

Today the only reminders of the Augustines are the pond which gives its name to one of the fences on the steeplechase course, and the Henry II Stakes. The race is named after the monarch who founded the original Priory when he wasn't having trouble with the Irish, tiresome bishops, fractious children and his finances; all familiar problems to those in government.

For the next few centuries, life alongside the Portsmouth road continued a casual rural existence. The paupers who occupied the old Priory buildings decided in 1740 that they would be more comfortable in the local workhouse; given the limitations of twelfth-century plumbing, this was clearly a wise decision, and Sandown became farmland and a recreation area for the people of Esher.

In 1870 the land came up for sale. Several schemes were mooted for development, including a lunatic asylum and a model village. No-one considered the idea of a racecourse except Lt. Col.

THE FIRST RACE FOR THE ECLIPSE STAKES, 1886 – BENDIGO WINS IN A RAINSTORM

Owen Williams of the Blues, a keen gambler and close friend of the Prince of Wales. Williams had the mixed fortune to own The Bard, a champion two-year-old. Unfortunately he was foaled in the same year as Ormonde, who beat The Bard by one-and-a-half lengths in the Derby on his way to complete the Triple Crown in 1886.

But the exploits of The Bard and Ormonde were more than a decade in the future at the time that Williams formed a consortium with a local squire, Sir Wilford Brett, and financed the purchase of the site. Owen Williams installed his brother, Hwfa pronounced 'hoofer', as manager

and proceeded to devise a revolutionary concept in racecourse management.

In the 1870s, there were few enclosures on racecourses; admission was charged for the grandstand, but the remainder of the course was open to all, including the roughest and coarsest members of late Victorian society, who by all accounts were even nastier than some of their current counterparts.

Naturally, the good citizens of Esher were dismayed at the prospects of their rural calm being shattered by frequent invasions of undesirables. They need not have worried; the Williams brothers' plans for Sandown were definitely up-market. The entire course was fenced in at a cost of £2,000, and a public stand and enclosure built, including catering facilities and separate ladies' and gents' loos. All this luxury cost half-a-crown for admission.

Meanwhile, the Members were also undergoing a reformation of their habits. They were all strictly vetted before membership was granted, as their behaviour record was in some cases worse than that of the proletariat. For the first time ladies were admitted to the Club as Members in their own right; hitherto, women could only enter a course as guests of gentlemen Members.

Gentlemen were also allowed two Ladies' Badges, and the influx of feminine company into what had been a largely male preserve had a sublime effect on the atmosphere. Now, women could go racing in complete safety, and Sandown soon became known as the first of the 'drawing-room' courses. Others were to follow, and as new courses were opened at Kempton, Lingfield, Plumpton, Haydock, Folkestone and Newbury in the next twenty years, all the enclosures were modelled on the Sandown pattern.

The first meeting in April 1875, presenting a mixed card of National Hunt and flat racing, was something of an anticlimax. The rain poured down, few people turned up, and no ruffian was discovered attempting to climb the ten-foot fence. However, the Members congratulated Hwfa Williams on his elegant, French-designed grandstand, Fred Archer rode a winner and most of the punters went home happy enough.

There was only one other meeting in the inaugural year, but the attendance of Owen Williams's friend, the Prince of Wales, not only set the seal on the venture from a social point of view, but also caused the erection of a Royal Box, originally made for Queen Victoria to review the Hyde Park Great Exhibition of 1851. The box was dismantled during the rebuilding of 1972 and now stands in a private park in Sussex.

Suitably encouraged, Hwfa Williams staged three summer fixtures in 1876, with a mixed meeting in the autumn.

By 1883 the *Illustrated Sporting and Dramatic News* had decided that Sandown Park 'is one of the pleasantest and most select and therefore most aristocratic of meetings, happily combining the 4 and 5 o'clock tea business and a charming spot for a picnic'.

The Williams policy of playing to the highest social denominator had paid off handsomely, and by 1886 Sandown could rival Ascot for smartness and sophistication. This was the year of the inaugural Eclipse Stakes, Hwfa Williams's finest brainchild. The race was supported financially by Leopold de Rothschild, and was worth £10,000 when the Derby was worth £4,600. It was the richest race ever run in Britain. For three-year-olds and upwards, it was run over Sandown's mile-and-a-quarter course.

Framed to attract only the best, even if a Derby, Oaks, St Leger or Grand Prix de Paris winner was penalised 10lb, it was no disgrace when the top-class handicapper Bendigo ran out the winner, beating among others in an outstanding field, the 1884 Derby winner St Gatien.

Bendigo was good enough to win the Champion Stakes in 1887, and was ridden in the Eclipse by his enthusiastic owner, Major Hedworth T. Barclay, known to his many friends as 'Buck'. This dashing Corinthian had broken more than one fair heart in the hunting country of Melton Mowbray when he celebrated his wedding a few weeks earlier, but he had advised all the guests to 'get on' Bendigo. Barclay had purchased the horse from Ireland for 750 guineas to give him a bit of fun in Hunters' flat races, though he was already the winner of the Cambridgeshire.

The Major never owned another really good horse, but after a distinguished career in racing he was present at Sandown in 1936 to see Rhodes Scholar win the Eclipse fifty years after the cheers had broken out for Bendigo.

Luck was not always on Hwfa Williams's side; he was shot by a madman whilst walking near his office in Pall Mall in 1883. But the Eclipse was his legacy to racing and to Sandown when he died in 1926 after fifty years in charge, even as he was planning a new course at Chepstow.

It is often said, and with truth, that it is impossible to compare generations in sport; who is to say, for instance, that Piggott was greater than Richards, or Richards superior to Donoghue, or Donoghue a finer champion than Archer? It can't be done; they were all supreme in their time, when in their prime. Similarly, it is extremely hard to quantify great races, except in one's own memory, usually too blurred by emotion to be properly analytical, notwithstanding the modern assistance of film and video.

In any case, the Eclipse defies analysis on any level, with such a montage of noble names. Ayr-shire, an easy winner of the Derby in 1888, won the Eclipse the following year. Orme cheated death in 1892 after being poisoned by a 'nobbler' when hot favourite for the Two Thousand Guineas, but recovered to win the Eclipse in successive years. Diamond Jubilee was a Triple Crown and Eclipse winner for the Prince of Wales in 1900 but in 1903 the Derby winner, Rock Sand, could finish only third to Ard Patrick and Sceptre; those three horses won seven classics between them. Coronach was the runaway winner in 1926, and Windsor Lad, beaten by untypical pilot error on the part of Charlie Smirke in 1934, came back to snatch a dramatic win in 1935 after breaking down two furlongs from home. Blue Peter, to be cheated of the Triple Crown by the outbreak of war, won in 1939.

Postwar, Charlie Smirke made no mistakes on Derby winner Tulyar in 1952, and H.M. the Queen's Canisbay got up by a whisker to beat Roan Rocket in 1965. Mill Reef majestically defeated Caro in 1971, but Mill Reef's Guineas conqueror Brigadier Gerard had to struggle in the mud which he hated, to beat the inferior Gold Rod in 1972. Pebbles became the first filly to win the Eclipse when she beat Rainbow Quest in 1985. Dancing Brave redeemed his reputation in 1986 and Mtoto was the first dual winner since Polyphontes in 1925 when winning in '87 and '88.

For the record, there has been one dead heat, in 1910, when Lemberg and Neil Gow reproduced their Two Thousand Guineas form almost to the ounce. Neil Gow had just got up on the Rowley Mile, and Lemberg had won the Derby.

During the 1914-18 war the course reverted to

agricultural use and the Royal Engineers utilised the stands, which had been rebuilt in 1903. In the twenties and thirties Sandown maintained its relentless up-market approach, spurning suggestions of inclusive rail travel and admission tickets and any dilution of the standards required for membership. Squawks of protest in the popular press fell on deaf ears; one complainant cited the admission charge, which was 150% higher for the public enclosure than at Hurst Park, but Hwfa Williams's policy of making racing popular without becoming populist continued to pay off and crowds of 40,000 attended the August Bank Holiday meetings.

Another Sandown success story is embodied in the National Breeders' Produce Stakes founded in 1889, and won by Pretty Polly in 1903, Neil Gow in 1909 and The Tetrarch in 1913. The 1913 race was clouded (in more ways than one) by controversy. It was a misty day, and the huge crowd assembled for the Eclipse meeting could not see the five furlong start on the two-year-old course, which bisects the round track at the furthest point from the stands.

The Tetrarch was already the winner of the Woodcote Stakes at Epsom, Ascot's Coventry Stakes and a Newmarket maiden when Steve Donoghue steered the spotted horse to post in the colours of Captain Dermot McCalmont of the 7th Hussars. As ever, The Tetrarch was keen at the start, too keen on this occasion, and as the field were called in for the first time, he got his nose over the tapes. Donoghue pulled him off the barrier, which was released a second later, and The Tetrarch cannoned into another runner, fell to his knees and was badly left.

Donoghue coaxed the horse home to win by a neck, all out. Many spectators, unaware of the drama at the start, thought the wonder horse was not so wonderful after all. The Tetrarch put the record straight with an easy win at Goodwood in the Rous Memorial, after which the racegoers on Trundle Hill pulled souvenir hairs from his tail as he trotted back to unsaddle.

The Tetrarch was never beaten, but he was unable to race after his two-year-old season and could not directly enhance the National Breeders' Produce Stakes as a classic trial, although he was to sire three St Leger winners and Tetratema, winner of the Produce in 1919 and the Two Thousand Guineas.

Between the wars, the race underlined the talent of many a champion, including The Tetrarch's daughter Mumtaz Mahal, Flamingo Myrobella, Colombo and Bahram. However, in 1939, the war clouds gathered again and racing at Sandown gave way to the Welsh Guards training battalion; but not before the infant B.B.C. Television Service had made a tentative request to show the Eclipse at a facility fee of £15. The stewards rejected the proposal, but were in a happier mood in 1947 when pictures from Sandown heralded the world's first live coverage of racing 'on the box', an innovation for which the author is profoundly thankful.

In the austere world of postwar socialist Britain, bread rationing was introduced; an unpopular measure which, as Winston Churchill was not slow to point out in the House of Commons, had not been necessary in the darkest days of

ECLIPSE DAY, 1925

THE WESTBURY STAKES WON BY BRIGADIER
GERARD (RIGHT, WITH JOE MERCER), 1972

the submarine war against the Atlantic convoys from America. Sandown did its bit, and an annual wheat crop was cultivated on the infield.

The lean forties gave way to the affluent fifties and sixties, and brought a danger far greater than the Luftwaffe, in the form of the property speculator. Sandown's old rival, Hurst Park, had succumbed in 1962, and the Esher course, already threatened with a by-pass, was extremely vulnerable with 160 acres of prime development land only fifteen miles from central London.

With attendances dwindling in the wake of the freshly legalised betting shops, shareholders in the racecourse company were keen to sell. Councils at local and county level were equally keen to oppose, as was the racing fraternity. A three-day Government enquiry held in the Members' Lounge was followed by a five-month hiatus while the Minister of Housing scratched his head and consulted his civil servants.

In the end, racing and the local people won the day. Embittered shareholders, robbed of their prize, merged the company with Epsom, and in turn the Horserace Betting Levy Board purchased both, together with Kempton. The three tracks are now administered on behalf of the Board by United Racecourses.

By now, the old stands were beginning to show their age, and shortly after Brigadier Gerard had passed the post to win the 1972 Eclipse, the bulldozers moved in to implement a £3,000,000 facelift including a cantilever grandstand with a capacity for 7,600 spectators. While work was in progress, Kempton played host to the Eclipse, won in 1973 by Scottish Rifle, ridden by Ron Hutchin-son. The following September, H.M. Queen Elizabeth the Queen Mother, performed the re-opening ceremony.

At first, the new stands of concrete and chrome received a hostile reception from the purists, but Sandown was facing the challenge of a modern world far removed from the drawing-room days of Edwardian elegance. In February 1980, former manager Edward Gillespie, now the distinguished racecourse manager at Cheltenham, addressed a meeting at King George's Hall, Esher, with these words: 'Not everybody liked it [the new stand], some hated it, some grew to it and others took to it straight away. But most important of all, the crowds have flocked to it, commerce and industry are attracted to it, private parties feel at home in it, and the "people" can watch good racing from it'.

I don't think 'Hoofer' could have asked for more. ∎

SALISBURY

IT IS an interesting fact that the most successful British politician in modern times, Margaret Thatcher, is disliked by some women because she is said to behave like a man. A similar criticism was also levelled at Mrs Thatcher's able and royal predecessor, Queen Elizabeth I – and I doubt whether either of them was unduly bothered by these vilifications. Of Elizabeth, an anonymous Frenchman wrote in 1603:

> Whilst Elizabeth was King,
> The English were of Spain the Terror
> But now, governed by Queen James:
> They only talk and prattle.
> (It rhymes better in French)

In May, 1588, Queen Elizabeth was on progress to see Sir Francis Drake for a final natter over the tactics for defeating the Spanish Armada, when she stopped off for a spot of racing at Salisbury. The feature race, for a Golden Bell value £50 and donated by her host, the Earl of Pembroke, was won by a horse owned by the Earl of Cumberland.

Once Drake had finished his bowling match and beaten the Spaniard too, with the assistance of a good public relations job by Gloriana at Tilbury, life resumed its easy way at the little racecourse high on Salisbury Plain and three miles from the Roman city of Sarum. In 1629, the Mayor and Corporation of Salisbury gave a Silver Cup to be run for at the spring meeting. Cheerfully ignoring the Civil War which had been raging for three years, including two battles at nearby Newbury, and doubtless encouraged by Cromwell's lack of success on either occasion, the church warden of St

Edmund's, Salisbury, recorded ringing in the races with the church bells, for which service he charged five shillings, and that 'Ye Erle of Pembrook his horse woon ye cuppe'.

Civil Wars over and Cromwell dead, racing flourished under Charles II. Much of the running being out of view, a man was stationed at the start to signal the commencement of each event with a musket shot. What effect this may have had on the runners is not recorded, but a 100 Guineas King's Plate was first contested in 1728, and victory went to the Duke of Bolton's Sweepstakes.

In 1765, the City Bowl, still on the card today, was inaugurated and won by Mr Larkin's grey aged horse Cyclops. Quite how good Cyclops was we cannot tell, but I doubt if he was as good as the 1768 winner, Gimcrack, or Eclipse who took the Bowl in 1769.

By the mid-nineteenth century, the meeting was in decline. Held on two days in August, the fields were suffering from the competition provided by the Bibury Club meeting at nearby Stockbridge. The Bibury Club is the oldest racing club in the world, tracing its origins to 1681, when Charles II was obliged to attend a Parliament at Oxford. Mistress Nell Gwyn found lodgings at nearby Burford, which was also handy for the racecourse at Bibury founded by James I about sixty years earlier. King Charles commanded that the King's Plate and other events be transferred from Newmarket for a series of meetings held on the track being used at the time by the Heythrop Point-to-Point.

After spells at Cheltenham and other venues, the Corinthians of the Bibury Club found what

STEVE CAUTHEN WALKS OUT FOR HIS FIRST
RACE IN BRITAIN, 1979

they hoped was to be a permanent home at Stockbridge in 1831. The card was principally for amateur riders, but also featured some good professional races, including the Champagne Stakes for two-year-olds, of thirty sovereigns each, colts to carry 8st 7lb and fillies 8st 4lb, with fifty pounds added by the club if three or more horses started. On the other hand, the winning owner was obliged to give 'three dozen of Champagne' to the thirsty club members.

Doubtless this conviviality contributed much to the success of the Stockbridge meeting, which may well have eclipsed the Salisbury fixture in time, but for the narrow-minded actions of a neighbouring landowner who refused to renew the lease on a small part of the course; perhaps he wasn't allowed to join the club.

In any event, the meeting described by F.H. Bayles as 'one of the best and most fashionable meetings we ever possessed, or are ever likely to possess, not to mention the loss to the small business residents of this quaint little Hampshire town, who looked forward with every natural pleasure to the profit accruing to them from this annual three-day fixture', came to an end in 1898.

Stockbridge was a favourite meeting of the Prince of Wales, and other personages described rather nicely by Bayles as 'big folks', and many a brave if breathless Corinthian went to his grave with memories of royal congratulations on his prowess in the pigskin. Accordingly the club lost no time in moving the fixture to Netherhampton Downs, the long established home of Salisbury, in 1899.

The new joint card provided a meeting in May, when the City Bowl was run together with the Salisbury Foal Stakes for two-year-olds and a National Hunt flat race over two miles. In July, the Bibury Club contributed, in addition to the usual races for amateurs, the Champagne Stakes and the Hurstbourne Stakes; both are still run today, although the Hurstbourne is a Nursery.

For many years, Salisbury had been an excellent proving ground for locally trained juveniles, and the Hurstbourne of 1899 was no exception. The winner, Elopement, trained at Kingsclere, went on to be fourth in the Two Thousand Guineas behind Diamond Jubilee. The tradition has continued, and many classic winners have shown their early paces over the plain, including Cameronian, Queenpot, Owen Tudor, Sun Chariot, Mill Reef and Brigadier Gerard, together with other top-class animals such as Fair Trial and Myrobella.

Between the wars, the Bibury Club continued their hospitable traditions, and the 'big folk' were able to enjoy lavish entertainment as five amateur races were run at the July meeting. The little folk didn't find it quite so amusing being crammed into Tatt's when the Biburians took over the club enclosure. Salisbury was one of the few courses to race during the war, but the austere atmosphere of postwar Britain saw the end of the Bibury, although it is remembered as the name on the badge of all Salisbury members.

Now, only the Carnarvon Challenge Cup survives to maintain the Corinthian spirit. It is not my intention to indulge in personal reminiscence, but I am reminded of the occasion when I visited Salisbury in the company of a former dis-

WINSTON CHURCHILL IN THE PADDOCK AT
SALISBURY, 1950

tinguished gentleman rider. As we ordered our drinks, he looked through his card and murmured, 'You know, the last time I saw the Carnarvon Cup, I rode the winner'.

As John Rickman reminds us in his *Homes of Sport*, Salisbury in the young summer sun is one of life's minor pleasures; but when the clouds are scudding, firmly secured wet weather gear is the order of the day. Such were the conditions when Steve Cauthen rode his first winner in England on Marquee Universal on 7th April, 1979. Less media attention was paid to a young man called David Elsworth enjoying his first winner on the flat on the same day as Steve with an ageing sprinter, Raffia Set. ∎

WINDSOR

'Every drop of the Thames is liquid 'istory.'
John Burns.

I F SO, more than a few gallons of the story of our sceptr'd isle have flowed past Windsor. Henry VIII raced the produce of his Hampton Court stud against animals owned by his cronies Sir Thomas Cheyney, Lord Kildare, Messrs Norrys and Karey and the Abbot of Glastonbury at Datchet and in the area now known as Windsor Great Park. King Hal was a keen punter, his 'black courser' running against 'Mr Karey's gelding for a wager'. The outcome of this contest is not recorded, but we do know that the King was a bad loser, Norrys receiving the attentions of the Tower Hill executioner following alleged adultery with Anne Boleyn, and the Abbot of Glastonbury 'judicially murdered' during the dissolution of the monasteries.

Charles II was an inveterate patron of the racing at Datchet Ferry, where he witnessed the meeting on 24th August, 1684, as he drained the last of his life's summer wine, and the meeting continued for many years although Queen Anne preferred the pleasances of Ascot Heath.

In 1866, the present course at Rays Meadow, then known as Clewer Meads, was opened on a Thames island close to 'Athens', a favourite bathing spot for Eton schoolboys. The track was designed by John Frail, of Frail Brothers, the celebrated racecourse administrators best remembered by the name of Cecil Frail. Many of the cognoscenti of the Turf were present at the first meeting on the 5th June, which was hardly surprising as Eton had celebrated Founder's Day on the

EVENING MEETING AT WINDSOR, 1979

4th; after a day indulging the family sprogs, what better than an afternoon at the races, or even two, as racing continued on the 6th.

The sport was never of high quality, but there was the odd highlight. Fred Archer, able to enjoy one of his rare good meals, won the £70 Surly Hall Welter Handicap over five furlongs on 7th April, 1876, partnering Aristocrat on his way to a then record 207 winners for the season.

Sixty-seven years later, on 26th April, 1943, Gordon Richards passed Fred Archer's total of wins, then considered to be 2,749, on a horse called Scotch Mist at Windsor; Scotch mist indeed, as Archer's aggregate is now known to be 2,748, and the record was already Richards's.

Windsor, in common with Manchester, Stockton, Brighton, Lewes, Birmingham and Newmarket, continued to race during the First World War, in spite of the usual outcry from the killjoys of both press and Parliament that the sport should be suspended in time of war. Lloyd George and his Government stood their ground and 'saw no reason to stop the very limited programme of racing which they have authorised and which is necessary to maintain the very important industry of horse breeding'.

Politics again played a part in the mid-twenties, when the Chancellor of the Exchequer, Winston Churchill, introduced an ill-conceived betting tax. Bookmakers at Windsor went on strike, an inaction which boosted the bar takings in all enclosures as the races were run in the silent presence of a few taciturn and frustrated punters.

The tax was swiftly removed from the Statute Book, and Windsor resumed its minor role on the racing stage, providing an attractive and undemanding venue for those seeking to retrieve losses on the Saturday following Royal Ascot. Even if the retrieval mission was unsuccessful, few could resist a consoling glass of champagne in Windsor's cool and leafy paddock.

As in the first global conflict, Windsor soldiered on through the 1939-1945 war, and in 1944 a doodlebug cut out immediately overhead, just as the jockeys were preparing to mount for the third race. Gordon Richards was riding for an amply-proportioned trainer called Vernel Hobbs, best described as early Jeremy Tree. Richards plunged into a flower bed in the centre of the parade ring and Hobbs landed on top of him.

As the champion jockey was examining himself for damage which felt worse than anything the Luftwaffe could have inflicted, Freddie Fox, who did not have a ride in the race and was watching from the stands, tartly observed to Jack Leach, on leave from the army, 'You should have seen those bookmakers throw themselves down on the ground. There wasn't a punter in the first fifty!'.

Peace returned to the Thames Valley to find Windsor in an innovative mood; a Ladies' Nomination private sweepstake was introduced. This was for two-year-olds bought at public auction in England for not more than five hundred and fifty guineas; the scale of subscription rose from twenty sovereigns for an animal purchased for a hundred guineas or less, to a hundred sovereigns for a yearling costing over four hundred guineas. As John Rickman observed, the ladies had a lot of fun at the sales, although in the author's experience, the ladies usually do.

Windsor

In 1947, severe flooding during one of the worst winters on record, cost £10,000. John Knight, who had joined Windsor in 1937 and eventually took over the management from the Frails, built a new weighing room and offices, and but for the bleak building restrictions of Britain's postwar Labour Government, he would have rebuilt the stands, inadequate even then, which survive today.

But not, perhaps, for much longer; Windsor's evening meetings, held on Mondays through the summer since 1964, consolidated their early success when Alexandra Park closed in 1970, and the charms of the riverside location brought Londoners by rail, and by road as the M4 opened up.

In March 1988, the course was sold to Thompson Investments; as I write, improvements to the tune of a million pounds are contemplated, and many would say, not before time. Nonetheless, some will regret the passing of the old, cosy Members' Stand. You couldn't see much of the running, but who cared? As John Rickman wrote in *Homes of Sport*, 'the distance from the Members' Bar to the bottom step of the Members' Stand is not as far as you can throw your hat'.

Only the first gentleman of televised racing could have written thus. ■

Bibliography

Books

Anon *Horse Racing: Its History* Saunders, Otley & Co. (1863).

Brock, D.W.E. *The Racing Man's Weekend Book* Seeley Service & Co. Ltd (1950).

Black, Robert *The Jockey Club and Its Founders* Smith, Elder & Co. (1891).

Burrows, G.T. *Cheshire Sports and Sportsmen* Phillipson & Golder Ltd. (1925).

Bayles, F.H. *Race Courses Atlas of Great Britain and Ireland* Henry Faux (1903).

Cawthorne, George and Herod, Richard *Royal Ascot* A Treherne & Co. Ltd. (1902).

Campling, Peter *The Park Courses* The Field Sports Press Ltd.

Curling, William *British Racecourses* H.F. & G. Witherry Ltd. (1951).

Cope, Alfred *Cope's Royal Cavalcade of the Turf* David Cope Ltd. (1953).

Donoghue, Stephen *Just My Story* Hutchinson & Co. (1923).

Dal Maso, Leonardo B. *Rome of the Caesars* Bonechi (1985).

Fairfax-Blakeborough, J. *Northern Turf History (Vols. III and IV)* J.A. Allen (1951).

Fairfax-Blakeborough, J. *Racecourses of Yorkshire* Reid-Hamilton Ltd.

Fawcett, William *Racing in the Olden Days* Hutchinson & Co. Ltd.

Fitzgeorge-Parker, Tim *100 Years of Kempton Park* United Racecourses Ltd. (1978).

Fletcher, J.S. *History of the St Leger Stakes* (1902).

Francis, Dick and Welcome, John *The Racing Man's Bedside Book* Faber & Faber (1969).

Fraser, Antonia *King Charles II* Weidenfeld & Nicolson (1969).

Fraser, Antonia *Cromwell, Chief of Men* Weidenfeld & Nicolson (1974).

Gilbey, Quintin *Fun Was My Living* Hutchinson & Co. Ltd. (1970).

Gilbey, Quintin *Champions All* Hutchinson (1971).

Gillespie, Edward *Kempton in Two Worlds Wars* United Racecourses Ltd. (1978).

Gross, John *The Oxford Book of Aphorisms* Oxford University Press (1983).

Gill, James *Racecourses of Great Britain* Barrie & Jenkins (1975).

Herbert, Ivor and Smyly, Patricia *The Winter Kings* Pelham Books (1968).

Leach, Jack *Sods I have Cut on the Turf* J.A. Allen (1961).

Leach, Jack *Rider on the Stand* Stanley Paul (1970).

Lucas, Pat *Fifty Years of Racing at Chepstow* H.G. Walters Ltd. (1976).

Marsh, Marcus *Racing with the Gods* Pelham Books Ltd. (1968).

Mortimer, Roger, Seth-Smith, Michael, Willett, Peter and Lawrence, John *The History of Steeplechasing* Michael Joseph Ltd. (1966).

Mortimer, Roger *Encyclopedia of Flat Racing* Robert Hale (1971).

Mortimer, Roger and Willett, Peter *More Great Racehorses of the World* Michael Joseph Ltd. (1972).

Mortimer, Roger, Onslow, Richard and Willett, Peter *Biographical Encyclopedia of Flat Racing* Macdonald & Jane's (1978).

Mortimer, Roger and Seth-Smith, Michael *Derby 200* Guinness Superlatives Ltd. (1979).

Mortimer, Roger (with Tim Neligan) *The Epsom Derby* Michael Joseph (1984).

Onslow, Richard *The Heath and the Turf* Arthur Barker Ltd. (1971).

Orton, John *Turf Annals* Thomas Empson (1844).

Rickaby, Bill *First to Finish* Souvenir Press Ltd. (1969).

Rickman, John *Homes of Sport* Peter Garnett Ltd. (1952).

Richards, Gordon (with Gerard Fairlie) *My Story* Hodder & Stoughton (1955).

Smith, Douglas (with Peter Willett) *Five Times Champion* Pelham Books (1968).

Smith, Eph *Riding to Win* Stanley Paul (1968).

Seth-Smith, Michael *Knights of the Turf* Hodder & Stoughton (1980).

Seth-Smith, Michael *Steve* Faber & Faber (1974).

Seth-Smith, Michael *Royal Triumphs at Kempton Park* United Racecourses Ltd. (1978).

Sidney, S. *The Book of the Horse* Cassell.

Sloan, Tod (edited by A. Dick Luckman) *Tod Sloan By Himself* Grant Richardson Ltd. (1915).

Siltzer, Frank *Newmarket: Its Sport and Personalities* London (1923).

Stevens, John *Knavesmire* Pelham Books Ltd. (1984).

Sutherland, Douglas *The Yellow Earl* Cassell (1965).

Tanner, Michael *The King George VI Steeplechase* Wayzgoose Ltd. (1984).

Trevelyan G.M. *English Social History* Longmans, Green & Co. (1944).

Welcome, John *The Cheltenham Gold Cup* Pelham Books Ltd. (1957).

Welcome, John *Fred Archer, His Life and Times* Faber & Faber (1967).

Wynn Jones, Michael *The Derby* Croom Helm Ltd. (1979).

Whyte, James Christie *History of the British Turf (Vols I and II)* Henry Colburn (1839).

Wright, Howard *The Encyclopedia of Flat Racing* Robert Hale Ltd. (1986).

Papers and Periodicals

The Sporting Life
The Racing Post
Horses in Training (1964-1988)
The British Racehorse
Ruff's Guide to the Turf
The Directory of the Turf
Timeform
Raceform
Baily's Magazine
The Tote Racing Annual (1965-1973)
The Racing Calendar (1727-1988)
Racing Illustrated (1896)
Bell's Life
Illustrated Sporting and Dramatic News
The Western Mail
The Scotsman
The Folkestone Herald
York Courant

Index

Index

PICTURE ACKNOWLEDGEMENTS

The author and publisher are grateful to the following sources for their help in providing the illustrations:

Illustrated London News 10, 11, 12, 25, 29, 41, 47, 53, 56, 58, 60, 61, 69, 71, 85, 92, 95, 97, 102, 104, 105, 107, 111, 113, 118, 120, 121, 123, 125, 126, 128, 129, 132, 133, 148, 155, 156, 157, 158, 161, 165, 169, 178, 179, 181, 185, 187, 188, 192, 193, 196, 198, 205, 206, 209, 214, 217, 219, 228 (inset), 231, 233, 234, 239, 245.

National Horseracing Museum, Newmarket 16, 49, 51, 117, 141, 203, 228.

British Museum 74, 75.

Gerry and Mark Cranham Jacket (front), 14, 63, 90, 103 (inset), 130, 138, 162, 171, 190, 206, 227, 243, 246.

Scottish National Portrait Gallery 19.

Scottish Tourist Board 23.

Sport and General 21, 135, 210, 222, 224, 240.

Carlisle Racecourse 31, 35, 37.

Hamilton Park Racecourse 31 (inset).

York Racing Museum 40, 77.

York City Art Gallery 79, 83.

Camera Press 221.